Channeled Fashion Tips from 33 Master Designers and Models

BOOK #4 IN THE CHANNELED MASTERS SERIES

Channeled Fashion Tips from 33 Master Designers and Models

Julie Bawden-Davis

Roses
ARE
RED
PUBLISHING

To my eternally elegant and beautiful mother, Lynn Kelley, a true fashionista. And to fashion lovers, models, and designers everywhere! May you find bliss in the infinite beauty of the world of fashion, with its incredible fabrics, colors, styles, designs, and endless possibilities for creating and experiencing splendor on Earth.

Acknowledgments

Many thanks to my daughter, Sabrina Wildermuth, for her absolutely perfect cover design. Thanks to my sister Mandy Stanley for her keen eye at proofreading. Much appreciation to Leslie Buckley, Charmaine Holland, and Melissa McFadden for advance reading. And thank you so much to all you Fashion Designers and Models for coming through me to share your inspiring and enlightening words about the beautiful, magnificent world of fashion. I am delighted and honored!

Stay Enlightened

Dear Enlightened Reader,

Thanks for reading! Let's stay in touch. In appreciation of you, I post updates, insider information, and sneak peeks of upcoming books on my website at www.juliebawdendavis.com/spiritual-coaching. You can also email me at Julie@JulieBawdenDavis.com, follow me on my Welcome to Ascension page on Facebook, and find me on Amazon.

Even better, you can join my VIP Enlightened Reader's mailing list here (eepurl.com/doM3-X) for weekly Divinely Inspired Channeled Messages just for you.

Author's Note

DEAR READER,

I must admit that while I've always admired beautiful clothing, and I even did a little modeling when I was a teenager, I wouldn't call myself a fashionista. I have a mother who is a fashionista, however, so I've been exposed to the beauty of the fashion world since childhood.

I and my three sisters spent many an afternoon crammed inside dressing rooms when we were young as mom tried on outfit after outfit. At the time I didn't understand why she would try on so much clothing and buy nothing or very little. (I was much more interested in the doughnuts she bought us after a shopping spree.)

Today, thanks to writing this book, I realize that it wasn't so much about the purchase. Although it was nice for mom to bring home new finds and enjoy wearing them, it all starts with the utterly delicious fun I now see she had trying on beautiful clothing. The excitement of spying a dazzling garment on the rack and running into the dressing room to try it on. Those moments as you tug on the garment and then look at yourself in the mirror. The victory of finding the perfect dress or pants or blouse. And the knowing that if the garment looked better on the hanger than you, there were oodles of other options to sample.

As I wrote this book, I had similar synchronistic experiences as I've had writing the other volumes. I would channel a fashion master's message and be astounded when writing the person's bio, which I always do afterward, rather than before, so I'm not influenced in any way.

For instance, when L' Wren Scott talked about perfume at length, I wondered why, because I knew her to be a designer. When I wrote her bio and discovered that she was responsible for Elizabeth Taylor's famed White Diamonds fragrance campaign, I understood why!

Other even more surprising things occurred. When I began to channel Jeanne Lanvin, I was thinking of the need to check on my dog, who hadn't been feeling well. Jeanne stopped me from starting her message and said, "Please go tend to your dog first. That is quite important." I thought it odd that a fashion designer should say that until I wrote her bio and discovered that she was an animal lover and in fact was photographed with dogs and cats.

I also found myself uncharacteristically concerned about my attire during the writing of this book. And I've received quite a bit of great fashion advice from the Light. When Christian Dior first came to me before I began writing this volume of the series, I was fretting over the fact that a new undergarment was literally coming apart at the seams.

Then I heard a voice say, "I know it is cliché, but they just don't make undergarments like they used to."

I replied that they didn't, and then the voice told me how to stop the seam from further damage until I could darn it later, as I was in a rush to leave the house. At this, I thanked the voice and asked, "Who are you?"

The response: "Why, Christian Dior, dear!" At that moment, I knew he was the project director for this book.

You will notice that all the designer and model masters are numbered. This is associated with numerology. They are in a certain order and given a certain number, as directed by those in the Light. Ages are also noted using numerals, as are some other numbers.

Keep in mind that there is a certain "language" coming from the Light. For instance, though you'll see that each entry has a different tone, rhythm, and character, there are some terms repeated, such as, so to speak, if you will, and truly. Such terminology allows those in the Light to announce themselves and confirm that it's them speaking.

If you question whether the words in this book are coming from each of the designers and models, that's your prerogative. Free will, which includes free thinking, is the law of the Universe.

Even so, I do hope you enjoy the tips and inspirations in this book regarding the gorgeous world of fashion. I know that it has opened my eyes to the beauty of clothing and jewelry and purses and shoes and glorious hair—the latter of which is one of my favorites.

Thank you also for reading. I and the Fashion Masters in the Light do appreciate it.

—JULIE BAWDEN-DAVIS

Channeled Fashion Tips from 33 Master Designers and Models

Introduction

HELLO! CHRISTIAN DIOR HERE. Yes, founder of Christian Dior! I am honored and grateful to be the project director for this book.

Thank you ever so much for taking the time to read this Channeled Masters volume. For taking the time to share your love of fashion with all of those in your life. For fashion is a most honorable profession, calling, and avocation.

Truly, loving fashion is the essence of loving yourself! Interesting way to put this, now isn't it? For let's be honest here. At times fashion is considered a bit shallow. And fashion is written off as not as important as other more weighty, vital issues—like global warming!

While I'm not here to minimize what might be seen as "bigger" issues, I am here to prove a point of sorts. While you can most certainly do your part to help the bigger issues, you can't solve all the world's problems in a moment's notice. Now can you?

However, you can most certainly quickly lift the spirits of yourself and others with fashion. I think you would agree when you consider how it's possible to feel a spring in your step when you dress up. Or, when you offer your services to one who might be less experienced and skilled in the fashion department. If the individual is willing and eager for your fashion tips and advice, why then, you can see the person light up at the mere mention!

That is what was so lovely for me as Christian Dior. During that life-time, I had the honor of presenting quite divine fashions to people—yet,

1

at the same time, these fashions were quite accessible to the average person. (We do laugh at that term here in the Light—for no one at all is "average.") But for the sake of this, I think you see of what I speak.

At any rate, I am honored as mentioned, to have been chosen to "lead" this book. And I and the other fashion experts here in the Light have had some fun with Julie as we've urged her to "try on" new fashions. We are also ever so excited to see what shall happen with all of you dear readers as this book does sprout wings and take flight!

I have digressed a bit. But that is certainly my prerogative from here in the Light—where time does stand still in a sense, and then speeds up, and then does return to a former time. A quite heady concept not to be covered here, but I do mention it for a reason.

The world of fashion does tend to make one look closely at time. I think you would agree. The world of fashion may even seem like a big ticking clock. What I am delicately tiptoeing around here is the concept of getting old in human years in your iteration of yourself at this time and in this place. What shall I tell you about this? Simply this. You ARE truly timeless. That being said, your choice of fashion can also be timeless. Am I suggesting that you wear a mini-skirt at the age of 80? No, I'm not necessarily, although there are certain ageless people who could pull that off! But I have given you this analogy to prove a point, so to speak.

You are ageless in your heart and mind. And you can choose whatever fashion makes you feel this way. So, if you do enjoy wearing long, flowing dresses, because they make you feel like a princess—please do! And if you like bowties—you guys and gals—why, then, wear bowties! You are you through and through, and that will shine through when you allow yourself to choose the fashions that you wish. I know this might sound a bit strange coming from me—who created a fashion line of the "latest" and "greatest." But I did do so with the idea in mind that all these fashions would give you ideas to create your own fashion sense. Your own unique you via fashion. That is a most glorious fashion show to watch. Your own!

Good day (or night) to you. Thank you again for listening. I and all of us in the Light Plane Fashion School so look forward to watching your fashion transformation!

Yours Truly,

Christian Dior

1

⇸ ANNA NICOLE SMITH ⇷

Hello! Thank you so much for having me! And number one! Oh, my! I am Anna Nicole Smith, and I am so pleased to present!

Present. Presentation. How is your presentation? How do you present yourself? Certainly, it seems a bit odd that now that us fashion and model masters are in the Light that we would be speaking to you about your human body. But then, you do live in your human body, don't you? And most likely, you'd like that human body to look its best? To present well?

So, I shall ask again—how do you present? And no worries, I'm not here to scold you about the state of your fingernails, or hair, or wardrobe. Rather, I'm here to talk about how you present. Because how you present has just as much to do with what is going on "inside" of you, as it is what is going on "outside" of you.

Certainly, you can look really "awesome," "stunning," and "incredible," if you don't feel all that great inside, but it will show in your eyes if you aren't feeling the same way inside. It truly, certainly will! And that will mar your overall appearance.

So, once again, how do you present?

If you are thinking that maybe I am speaking of an "inside" job here, I most certainly am. I can tell you this now that I am here and not as fixated, shall we say, on every hair being in place, that it is about the outer being—of course—but what is going on inside is just as important.

Can either one of these two "things" be more important than the other? No, not really. I'm not going to tell you in a book of fashion advice that your outsides don't matter at all, as long as your insides are shining! That would certainly be a bit silly, and quite frankly not true in the fashion realm. But I can tell you that as you are working on your appearance—your presentation—that it would be an equally good thing to also look carefully at your insides. To shine a bright, bright flashlight into your insides. A flashlight infused with good intentions, of course, but also fairy dust! Yes, the fairies are most happy to help you with your inside and outside presentation. All you need do is ask!

As you shine the flashlight inside and light up the dark corners, you will feel a sort of release at that point. A release because you will be aligning your insides with your outsides. And that is a splendid thing, as we say from here!

Okay, so you might have thought I would give you some tips for how to look utterly gorgeous and desirable. Some practical tips, like the brand of lipstick or eyeliner, or the way you apply these. I most certainly have such tips!! And I shall give you some of those tips. Now that I've given you my "take" on how important it is to let your insides shine through onto your gorgeous outsides. For then you will truly be a diamond of a beauty!

When applying your eyeliner—do take a hard line, if you will, at the corners. It is there in the corners of your eyes that you want to make the bold statements. I know you've seen this method used amongst many other beauties, like my good friend dear Marilyn (#2). Then do taper off with the eyeliner as you move inward away from the corners of your eyes. Make it a precise tapering. That is the secret! (And yes, this does take some patience and time!)

And your lips. Do watch the color of the lipstick you choose. Do match the lipstick as closely as possible to your outfits. This can simply mean matching it to a scarf you are wearing, or a color in a print you are wearing. It is quite easy to do and does give you a complete presentation!

Thank you, once again, for listening to me! I do hope you have fun with fashion. I do! For fashion is so utterly glorious—and does make you look and feel like the beautiful being you truly are!!
   Kisses and Hugs Always!
   Anna Nicole Smith

ANNA NICOLE SMITH (Vicky Lynn Hogan) was an American model, television personality, and actress born on November 28, 1967. She died at the age of 39, due to an accidental drug overdose, on February 8, 2007. Smith earned fame as a model for Guess and as the *Playboy* magazine 1993 Playmate of the Year. She also modeled for fashion companies such as H&M, Lane Bryant, and Heatherette. Smith was born in the small town of Mexia, Texas. She grew up without a father and married her first husband at 17, giving birth to a son, Daniel, when she was 18. (Her son later died of an accidental overdose on September 10, 2006.) Smith always dreamed of becoming the next Marilyn Monroe (#2), so she left her son in the care of her mother and went to work in a Houston strip club. There she met the Texas oil tycoon J. Howard Marshall, whom she married in 1994. He died the following year in 1995, and Smith spent many years in court regarding his estate. In 1992, she mailed photos of herself naked to *Playboy* and was invited to pose for the magazine. The following year, she became Playmate of the Year. This led to some small film roles, as well as a great deal of attention from celebrity magazines.

2

➤ MARILYN MONROE ➤

Hello there! Marilyn Monroe here! Very happy to present here. There was some talk regarding if I should appear in this or the upcoming volume on actresses. My role as a "beauty" in my life as Marilyn did squarely "land" me in this book, however!

Beauty. Even the word brings up various images, doesn't it? What do you hold dear? What do you hold as beautiful? At first glance, this does appear to be a rather simple question. For you do have your checklist for what is considered beautiful in your day today! A certain look to the face—a certain width, even, between the eyes. A certain plumpness, shall we say, to the lips.

Oh, my, it is a bit overwhelming, isn't it, to consider what is considered beautiful!

Do you feel overwhelmed by all of this? Do you look in the mirror and feel a bit dismayed when you think of all that you need to do to "make" yourself beautiful? Is it a burden at times?

I did so enjoy the fashion aspects of being Marilyn—for we can be honest from here in the Light—I did have A LOT to work with!! But there were times when the beauty was a bit of a burden. Is this to say that you should simply throw your hands up and give up! Certainly not! Unless you want to, of course. I'm only mentioning that even "great beauties" such as me as Marilyn do find it a bit overwhelming at times to keep up with the image of beauty.

You notice I used the word image. For truly, it is an image that you create when you create your own signature style. And while I'm certainly not suggesting you don't do this—I am letting you know that it is a bit of work, as you may be seeing.

At the same time, you do have a bit of a conundrum in your day and age. For "being beautiful" and doing all that is required to look beautiful and to fulfill the image you create is sometimes considered a "shallow" task. There are much better things to do, you may hear, such as save the rainforest or worry about alarming events occurring in the world!

I am not here to disparage any efforts to save any rainforests—for certain cosmetics even have their origins there! I only make this analogy to show you that there are some forces working against you when it comes to making yourself look beautiful.

And yet, the world so loves a beauty, doesn't it?! The camera literally eats up the various images of those beauties. The public longs to see photo after photo of beauties of your day and beauties of the past, such as me and others you will find in this book.

What am I saying here, you may be wondering?

This is what I wish to impress on you. You are a beautiful creature—you simply are!! And it is quite alright—it is, in fact, your birthright—to make yourself as beautiful as you wish. To create your own signature image and style, and to be proud of that image and style! You doing this for yourself is equally as important as another person's top priority, which could be saving the rainforest or writing a gigantic book of knowledge!

No one action is any "better" than another! And there truly are no "shallow" actions. I would like, if you choose, that you dismiss any of these thoughts. So, do beautify yourself in whatever manner you wish—and don't feel guilty doing so!

Whatever method you choose to make your signature beauty mark I will say hooray to! For whatever you do will be coming from deep within you—the real you—and you can't help but shine like a bright, bright diamond when you do this! And we all know that diamonds are a girl's (or guy's) best friend!

Good day to you. Thank you ever so much for listening. I do look forward to standing behind you as you look in the mirror—at lovely you, you, you!!
Kisses!
Marilyn Monroe

NORMA JEANE MORTENSON (Marilyn Monroe) was an American model, actress, and singer born on June 1, 1926. She died at the age of 36, due to a drug overdose, on August 4, 1962. Monroe is considered one of the most beautiful women of all time. Often referred to as a "blonde bombshell," she possessed many of the hallmarks of great beauty, including an hourglass figure and breathy voice. She segued from modeling into acting, becoming a top-billed actress for more than a decade. Monroe had a difficult childhood. She was born in Los Angeles, where she spent most of her childhood in foster homes and an orphanage. She married at 16 during World War II. It was while working in a factory during this time that she was introduced to a photographer and ended up becoming a successful pinup model. This eventually led to contracts with Twentieth Century-Fox and Columbia Pictures. In the mid-1950s, she founded her own production company, Marilyn Monroe Productions, because she was tired of being offered strictly "dumb blonde" roles. Monroe was married three times. Her second marriage was to baseball star Joe DiMaggio and her third to playwright Arthur Miller. During her honeymoon with DiMaggio, she was asked to perform for American servicemen in Korea, which she did in February 1954. She appeared onstage in a sparkling purple dress in freezing temperatures, doing 10 shows in four days, which led to her developing pneumonia. Despite becoming ill, Monroe said that those performances were the best thing that ever happened to her and made her feel like a "star" in her "heart." Monroe was also known for her generosity. She was especially generous to children. She gave to organizations such as March of Dimes and Milk Fund for Babies.

3

➤ YVES SAINT LAURENT ◆

Hello there, Yves Saint Laurent here. Most honored and truly happy to present! I shall do my best to enlighten you about fashion and the fashion world!

The fashion world. What a glorious one!! For where on the Earth can you be surrounded by such beauty! Such fluid, ever changing, flowing beauty! Clothing, attire, apparel, accessories. Why, my, oh, my, all these elements do bring forth a beauty like no other! And of, course, the lovely models—some of whom are included in this group—do highlight all these elements and more. Let us not forget gorgeous hair, as it flows down a female back and does highlight the clothing as well.

What am I speaking of here? Why, certainly, I am speaking of clothing, and all that it represents. Yet so much more! For fashion truly is beauty. Fashion is the sheer representation of beauty in all its life forms! I so did love beauty, beauty, beauty during my life as Saint Laurent. I most certainly did. Beauty to look at, most certainly, and beauty to adorn.

What shall I tell you now that I've waxed on about beauty? We could discuss so much in the fashion realm! Yet I will reign things in, as you might say, and focus on a few things that I am feeling compelled to share at this time with you dear readers.

Your beauty. Your own beauty. Your own elegant form. Your own elegance. That is what I would like to discuss with you. For I do see from here many of you on the Earth Plane, who do struggle with internalizing their own magnificent beauty. Your beauty, I must tell you, does shine "up here" so brightly that we are certainly blinded on many occasions—as we can be blinded from here!

But I do wish to assure you that you are beautiful through and through. You most certainly are! And the more you put into your beauty "arsenal," shall we say—such as blushes and lipsticks and mascaras and purses and shoes and evening gowns and blouses, and for men trousers and cufflinks, etc.—the more you shine. Does this mean that you should get more and more and more of these things? Well, certainly, if you choose to, please do! But to answer that question, no, you needn't have much. For truly, beauty is more than skin deep, yet beauty is skin deep. I know this sounds rather confusing, but then again, I think you do know of what I speak.

We have so far ascertained that it is quite alright to add to your beauty arsenal when you so choose. And that you are a beauty, no matter what. For beauty does reside in the soul and beauty does reside in what you do bring into your life—that which is beautiful.

That brings up my next point. What you see as beautiful. Do take up what you see as beautiful when possible and do wear it with your own personal style and flair! I say this now from here, because I can. What you choose to wear doesn't have to be "in style," unless of course that is what you desire. I say this because I wish for you to wear what makes you feel beautiful. Be it from last season or even a decade ago!! For when you wear what makes you feel beautiful, you do add to your beauty arsenal and you shine even brighter!

What more can I tell you? Do be comfortable in your clothing. Of course, there will be times when you will wear something that is a bit constraining, because you just love it! However, it is not necessary to be uncomfortable to be beautiful. Somewhere along the way, this concept became *de rigueur*. Most likely with women's shoes. I won't go into detail with that, for I do know that another will appear to discuss shoes at great length. Just suffice it to say that comfort and appearing comfortable is another sign of sheer beauty. Comfort in your clothing leads to comfort in your skin, which leads to beauty through and through!

That is all from me for now. I do hope that I have given you some essential and useable input, as they say. And I do hope that I've convinced you that your beauty shines through—always!!
Good Day to You and Blessings,
Yves Saint Laurent

———————— ❦ ————————

YVES HENRI DONAT MATTHIEU SAINT LAURENT (Yves Saint Laurent) was a European fashion designer born on August 1, 1936. He died at the age of 71, due to brain cancer, on June 1, 2008. Saint Laurent is well known as being one of the most influential fashion designers of the last several decades. He revolutionized the fashion industry in a variety of ways, including making ready-to-wear viable, as well as fashionable. Saint Laurent was born in Oran, French Algeria to Charles and Lucienne Andrée Mathieu-Saint-Laurent. He recalled when he was alive having great childhood memories of growing up in Oran with his two younger sisters. His parents would have dinner parties, and he enjoyed it when his mother would come to his room to wish him goodnight, dressed in a long white tulle dress bedecked in sequins. Saint Laurent had few friends at school. Instead, he found comfort in the world of fashion. He started out creating intricate paper dolls and by his teens designed dresses for his mother and sisters. When he was 17, his mother took him to meet the editor of *French Vogue* in Paris. Saint Laurent moved to Paris the following year to attend Chambre Syndicale de la Couture, where he and his designs quickly became noticed. Saint Laurent was also introduced to Christian Dior (#33), whom he credited with teaching him the basics of the art of fashion. At first, he did simple tasks for Dior, eventually submitting sketches to the designer, who often used them. Dior chose Saint Laurent to succeed him. This occurred when Dior died of a heart attack when Saint Laurent was just 21. By 1966, Saint Laurent launched his own fashion label. His adaptations of men's attire for women, such as tuxedos and blazers, gained him fame. In 1983, Saint Laurent was the first living designer to have a solo exhibition in New York's Metropolitan Museum of Art.

———⌘———

"Fashion dies, but style remains."
—*Yves Saint Laurent*

4

✦ Gianni Versace ✦

Hello there! Nice to present in this marvelous work! Gianni here. At your "fashion tips" service.

Fashion, fashion, fashion!!! Oh, I just so love the word. I certainly could almost gobble up the word, even, as Gianni. For the fashion world is a most magnificent world! One can truly invent oneself with fashion. That is one of the most auspicious elements of all of this. Inventing yourself. Inventing your true look! Hooray!!

What shall I tell you today, as I take advantage of this chance to say my piece, as they say?!

Well, firstly, I would like to say that I would like you to focus on just this. Saying your piece. Your own piece. Through fashion, glorious fashion. Display the true you when you clothe yourself and add the various accessories. For doing this will certainly show others the true you—the true you clothed and accessorized as you wish to clothe and accessorize!

Okay, so I have gotten that off my proverbial chest, as they say. Now what shall I tell you?

I shall share with you a few fashion tips. Advice that will allow you to be the absolute most gorgeous—or handsome—you!

1. Follow your heart. I know, I do sound rather strange saying this—given that as Versace I did have my own thoughts about all of this. But here from the Light I must tell you that your heart must truly sing for you to look your absolute best. That being said, I do encourage you to wear what you wish (within reason, of course!) But do wear what makes your heart full of joy!

2. Embrace your bliss. Whatever it is you do in your life that does make you happy, embrace it. This will make whatever you wear look fabulous—be it a burlap sack. Although, please know I am using this as an analogy only! When you are blissful, truly, whatever you wear will look absolutely divine!

3. Accessorize. I know I jump around a bit here. Forgive me! But, yes, accessories do complete the picture, as they say. They do put the proverbial icing on the ensemble. So, do pay particular attention to your accessories. Not only their colors, but also their shapes and sizes. If you are wearing, for instance, a dress with a small print pattern, do choose a purse that is also small in size. In the same respect, if you are wearing a pattern that contains ovals or rectangles, do choose earrings that have the same patterns and shapes to them. I do think you are seeing what I am saying here!

4. Lipstick. Others in this volume will speak of lipstick, but I will also say my "schtick about lipstick!" The color, the shades. They do matter. There, quite frankly, is a good reason why the makers of cosmetics spend ample time and energy and money on the various shades of lipstick! So, do take advantage of the various shades. Know that the shade you choose does matter. A shade that is just a touch different than another shade may be the ideal shade for your ensemble and your face and coloring and eyes, even!

5. Mascara. Wear mascara as you can. By this, I mean that if you only wish to put on a little, then do so. The point is to play up your lashes, which will then play up your eyes. I assure you! Do take care with the shade of your mascara, as well. Brown is most certainly a much better shade for those with fair skin and light hair than black.

6. How your clothing "falls" on you. Back to the clothing, of course!! The clothing you choose will look its best if it falls on your form in such a way that it looks relaxed, yet as if the clothing is also standing slightly at attention. This is a concept that you may understand now, or you may have to see after reading this. Do put on your favorite outfit—and do see how the clothing falls on your form. You will most likely see that it does look casual in terms of fitting and jiving with you, yet it does have a bit of a perk to it that does hint at the fact that you are up for a bit or a lot of excitement when you wear the outfit!

Okay, I've babbled on quite a bit. I do hope this all helped you!
Always Yours,
Gianni Versace

———— ⌘ ————

GIANNI VERSACE was an Italian fashion designer born on December 2, 1946. He died at the age of 50, due to a gunshot wound, on July 15, 1997. Versace is the founder of Versace, an international fashion house producing clothing, accessories, makeup, fragrance, and home furnishings. He also designed costumes for films and the theater, which allowed him to embrace his penchant for bold colors, accessories, and drapery. Versace befriended a wide variety of musicians, including Elton John, Cher, Eric Clapton, and Sting. These connections linked music to the fashion world. Versace was born in Reggio Calabria, Italy to an appliance salesman father and seamstress mother. He didn't like school, preferring to be in his mother's workshop, where she made wedding dresses. She would suggest he play outside with friends, but Versace told her he wanted to learn how to make clothes. Versace became famous in his mid-twenties in Milan, where he designed provocative and fun clothing designed to attract attention. He excelled at marketing his fashion line. He was one of the first to use rock stars and actresses in his campaigns. He was also gifted at spotting and nurturing new talent and is credited with the creation of the super-model. Versace employed his family in his company, including his sister, Donatella, and his brother, Santo, who remained involved in the company after their brother's death. Versace was shot by a serial killer outside of his home.

5

❖ JOI LANSING ❖

Hello there! Joi Lansing here. A former model/beauty, as they say, in "my day." Let's talk beauty and fashion!

Beauty, beauty, beauty. Even the name is, well, beautiful! I so loved the beauty and fashion industry as Joi. I did! The glamour, the fashion, the everything—especially back in the days that I was active in Hollywood!

Of course, things were different back then. A gal, if she decided to jump in and let people know she existed, could be heard. Today there are many in the fray, so to speak, so getting noticed in the fashion industry can be quite challenging. In the same respect, you have so much at your disposal now to make yourself ultra-glamorous, and to display your many unique talents!

I do wish to be of some service to you, and so I shall "talk" here about getting yourself noticed. For this is most certainly one of the first steps to fashion fame, now isn't it?

Here are some tips from me to you. And I am keeping in mind the day and age in which you are traversing! That way these suggestions will be ever so fresh and useful to you!

Be yourself. I know this has already been said before in this book, and no doubt, it will be said again and again. But I urge you to be yourself. Does this mean that you act as you do with your mother or siblings or father or other loved ones? Well, not exactly. Of course, there are those "sides" of you that you don't necessarily wish to share. But I do mean to show your very essence. To be vulnerable enough to show what makes you—you!

Fine, now what, you may ask?

Listen to others, yet, also listen to yourself. This is a quite important point that I do hope you internalize, if you so choose! You know what you wish to do, and you know that you are indeed a beauty in your own right—be you male or female! (I am speaking to male models here, as well!) It is quite fine to listen to other's suggestions and tips and tricks, but please, I do implore you, ignore any comments about what is "wrong" with you, or what you are "lacking." I truly tell you this now that those sorts of tidbits are not helpful—they are rather a hindrance! There have been so many times that such barbs have stung so badly that raw talent is subdued and may give up! So, do ignore anything that comes slung at you in the guise of "helping," but stings when it jabs you!

You do know, I am sure, how fragile are the egos of great beauties. Like thin, thin glass! That is why the former suggestion is so important for you to believe and internalize. At the same time, you do want to thicken your glass. Don't you! That way when those barbs are flung at you as you become more successful, they will simply bounce off onto the floor. You shall walk around or even on them without a care in the world about them! Believing in yourself first and foremost will help you thicken your glass.

Any tips and tricks, I do hear you asking, for making yourself as gorgeous (or handsome!) as possible? Certainly. A quick list for you!

Poise and grace. This comes from good posture. Do pay careful attention to your posture. Please do!! Do walk about with books on your head or whatever it takes to get you to stand up straight and with ease.

Dressing elegantly. Dressing elegantly does not necessarily mean dressing flamboyantly. It is quite often the opposite. If you are striving for elegance, you will want to dress down some. Not in work clothes or anything—but the added necklace you are considering when you already have one on can most likely be reserved for the following day's outfit. The pumps you choose—the shoes—they are also of consequence. Mix a bit of flair with a bit of attractive conservativism, and you shall have elegance.

I mentioned your shoes. Do pay careful attention with how they "jive" with your outfit. There are dresses that just beg for high heels, while there are others that could take a moderate heel, or a wedge, or flat, even. You will know when you try on the various shoes with the outfit. So, yes, trying on all those shoes is a must.

Your hair. Do wear your hair as you love your hair. At the same time, do try to get some volume out of your hair—for the flat against the head look is not all that attractive on film—in males or females.

Do have fun! I know this seems a rather "funny" thing for me to add. But when you are having fun, your smile will be bright and gorgeous. It truly will!

> *That is all from me for now. I hear a little rumbling that I've taken up quite a bit of space here—but that is okay, as they say. For that brings me to my last suggestion. Do take up the space you are meant to with your fine form and bright smile and elegant attire. You are urged to command the space you are given—that will most certainly serve you well in the fashion realm as a model or trendsetter.*
>
> *Good Day Always!*
>
> *Joi Lansing*

JOYCE RAE BROWN (Joi Lansing) was an American model, actress, and nightclub singer born on April 6, 1929. She died at the age of 43, due to breast cancer, on August 7, 1972. Lansing is best known as a pin-up model and for various roles in movies of the 1950 and 1960s. This included an opening appearance in *Touch of Evil*, Orson Welles' 1958 crime drama. Lansing's modeling career was busy and successful during the 1940s. Though she often appeared in skimpy outfits, Lansing was a devout Mormon and didn't pose nude. She practiced yoga for relaxation. Lansing was born in Salt Lake City, Utah to a father who sold shoes and played in an orchestra. Her mother was a housewife. The family moved to Los Angeles in 1940, and she began professional modeling soon after at the age of 14. She completed high school on the studio lot while working for MGM.

6

Hello and bonjour. I am Coco Chanel, and I am honored to present here. Thank you for listening/reading, as they say!

Oh, my, what a glorious, glorious work! I am honored, as I have said, to present, and I do wish to be of assistance, and so I shall do my absolute best!

The fashion life. What a glorious one it is! For where on the Earth can you access the physical beauty of something to such an extent. For certainly, the fashion realm "allows" and even calls for you to enjoy beauty and beautiful things—be that people and fabrics and the cut of a dress and the feel of soft leather and fur on the skin!! And then the jangle of precious jewels as they swing from an ear as an earring or are corralled into a necklace and placed around one's neck or wrist or ankle!

I did so enjoy fashion as Coco. I so did! But that is most likely obvious, I would think! At any rate, let us talk about being a fashion designer, shall we? I do think that I have something or more than something to say along those lines.

So, you want to be a fashion designer? What should you do? How should you prepare? Well, fashion design school would be a good first step. Surely. Choose a reputable school, and there are many in this day. As you choose which school you would like to attend, do go for the school that makes your heart excited—makes your heart sing a bit. For that is your soul's/intuition's way of telling you that the school is for you.

When you get to the school, when you are accepted, do take advantage of everything and anything that you can! Even if you don't think you shall be going into men's fashion, for instance, do study the ins and outs of men's fashion, anyway. Study as if you are going into men's fashion, even. This will give you a breadth of study that will serve you well as you navigate the fashion design world. I assure you!

Let me use an analogy of being a teacher here to explain what I am saying. You may eventually settle on teaching junior high students. However, possessing the knowledge of what they learned before and what they will soon learn is of vital importance to your mastery of the teaching profession and your usefulness to the students you have.

Focus on patterns. Physical patterns. Look at "old-school" physical patterns and designs and drawings and do examine them. Take them apart, even, to see how they were put together. I say this to you now and it may seem unnecessary, but I assure you that knowing how the pattern came to be will teach you much! For one, it will teach you about the inner workings of the designer who did put the pattern together. At the same time, it will teach you how to put together your own designs. To go from the image of a piece of clothing you have in your head to the pattern on the page that will enable that piece of clothing to become a reality.

I think you see what I am saying, *n'est-ce pas?* Strive for accuracy with your patterns, as well. Be brutal with your approach to accuracy. For the slightest variation in a pattern can cause a wrinkle here or a loose fit there, and that can literally throw off the elegance of the entire garment!

Use folds and gathered effects judiciously. What may seem like a good idea in your mind's eye can look rather unattractive when overdone in the patterns and translated to the garment. Clean, straight, flats lines often look the best on the human form. Of course, every human form is different. That is when special effects may work quite well.

That being said, do study the human form—it's many lines and curves, and even its limits. For that will teach you much about designing. In fact, an anatomy class would be a quite good addition to your course of study.

What else shall I say before I end?

Simply this. If you wish to be a fashion designer, you most certainly can and will be one! You just will. For the hunger for fashion does wash through the body and must be expressed in one way or another! And if you have chosen your way as a designer, then the world most certainly won't stop you! In fact, the only person who may stop you is you—with imagined limitations. There are no limits! If you feel you are a fashion designer at your core and heart, then you most certainly are!

I shall see you in the Fashion Design & Modeling School in the Light—where you can go at night while you sleep, if you so choose! You need only ask when you lay your head down on your pillow.
Yours,
Coco Chanel

————∞∞∞————

GABRIELLE BONHEUR "COCO" CHANEL was a French fashion designer and entrepreneur born on August 19, 1883. She died at the age of 87, due to a heart attack, on January 10, 1971. Chanel is widely known as one of the most revolutionary fashion designers of all time. She refused to follow trends and is responsible for liberating women from corseted clothing that prevailed prior to World War I. Her elegantly casual designs inspired women to abandon petticoats and corsets for more comfortable attire. Chanel is the founder and namesake of the Chanel brand, including the signature perfume Chanel No. 5. (A fortune teller told her that 5 was her lucky number.) In addition to couture clothing, characterized by its sporty, chic style, she designed jewelry, shoes, handbags, and hats. Chanel even created her iconic CC monogram. She is also responsible for introducing the "little black dress" in 1926. The fact that the dress was black—a color used only for mourning at that point—was revolutionary in itself. Chanel was *Time Magazine's* only fashion designer to make the list of the 100 most influential people of the 20th Century. She was born in a convent-run orphanage where the nuns taught her to sew. She acquired the name Coco when she began singing in cafes as a young woman. She often sang the songs "Ko Ko Ri Ko" and "Qui qu'a vu Coco." In 1913, she opened her first business—a small millinery shop in Deauville, France. By the late 1920s, Chanel industries was worth millions and employed more than 2,000 people. Today, there are more than 300 Chanel stores worldwide.

———— ✺ ————

"Luxury must be comfortable, otherwise it is not luxury."
—Coco Chanel

7

⇒ Oscar De La Renta ⇐

Hello there, and greetings! Oscar de la Renta here, at your Light Plane Fashion service!

The beauty of the female form! My, oh, my, how I loved to gaze on the beauty of the female form during my life as Oscar. For the female form does lend itself to utterly divine designs! It so utterly does.

This is something I shall like to discuss today. The beauty of the female form and letting the female form guide you as you design. For truly, you are designing for the female form—and so she shall be your best guide!

Of course, there is the male form. I don't wish to sound as if I am dismissing the male form. Rather, I am just commenting on the fluidity and grace that is the female form in all its forms! The male form certainly does have its place in the fashion realm! And there are other designers here who will most certainly discuss male fashion. So, I shall go back to what I was most decidedly "good" at clothing during my life as Oscar—the female form!

Where shall we go with this? The female form? Let me suggest that you do tap into the female form, even if you aren't looking directly at one when you are designing. Rather, I suggest that you tap into the energy of the female form—to its fluidity and enduring grace. For when you do this, you will find that your designs do come rather easily. In fact, they will come with full force at times. The design will take you by the throat, as they might say, until you sit down and relay the design to the page or computer screen. Until then, it simply won't let you go!

What shall you do once you have the design down on paper or computer? Sit back and relax? Well, you could for a short spell. But then I do urge you to go ahead and take a good long, hard look, as they say, at the design. When you do this, cast all judgment aside. Simply stare at the design until the dress or skirt or blouse or entire ensemble begins to move and makes its way to clothe a glorious female form.

Watch as the model in your mind's eye does dance about in the outfit and model it for you. Then do look at the imaginary model's face. Is she smiling? Do her eyes sparkle with joy? For if they do, you have a winner, my dear Light Plane Fashion student!! For the models in your mind's eye will let you know when a design is utterly Divine! (I so love how that rhymes!)

What else? Well, what if the model is not smiling? What if she has a raised eyebrow, let's say. This could mean that there is an aspect of your design that certainly should be tweaked so that the model then smiles. Is the sash around the midriff of the dress too tight? Or does it appear too frilly? Or should it be removed altogether? Perhaps the hemline is a bit too short, or a bit too long? Do pay careful attention if your imaginary model does raise her eyebrow or eyebrows.

Of course, your imaginary model might just frown. Oh, my! This is a "warning" of sorts, wouldn't you say? Or at least an alert. For when this is done, it means there is something amiss with your design. So, do take a good look at the design. But when you do, I suggest you do look at the design like this: Glance quickly and then shut your eyes. Open them quickly again. What do you see during these glimpses? Most likely, something is going to jump out at you. Whatever does jump out at you is what requires your attention. It could be the planned print of the dress, or it could be the material you wish to you use, or it could be the collar. Whatever it is, take notice! Do a little re-designing, and then let your model get dressed again and see if she smiles!

That is all from me for now. I do feel as if I've babbled a bit here, but then, on second look, I do see that I have given you some good fashion design tips! You shall most likely find you have a similar experience with your own work. At first you may feel as if you have no idea what you just designed. You may think that certainly it is rambling sketched on the page. Yet, on second look you will find that your design is absolutely divine!

Thank you dearly for listening to me! I am deeply honored and very excited to see this book come to fruition.
    Yours Sincerely,
    Oscar de la Renta

ÓSCAR ARÍSTIDES RENTA FIALLO (Oscar de la Renta) was a Dominican-American fashion designer born on July 22, 1932. He died at the age of 82, due to complications of cancer, on October 20, 2014. De la Renta is considered one of the world's leading fashion designers. He is famous for blending the luxury of European fashion design with the casual comfort of American fashion, creating decidedly flattering and feminine designs. He became internationally known when he dressed Jacqueline Kennedy. He also dressed many other first ladies, including Nancy Reagan, Hillary Clinton, and Laura Bush. De la Renta was born into a middleclass family in Santa Domingo, Dominican Republic. He had six sisters. De La Renta studied painting in Madrid, Spain. While he initially considered becoming a painter, fashion design lured him. His ability to draw got him an apprenticeship with renowned Spanish couturier, Cristóbal Balenciaga. He began working in fashion in Paris, then moved to New York to join the American design house of Elizabeth Arden (#8). By 1965, he had started his own ready-to-wear line that effused casual luxury. De la Renta also marketed his clothing in Latin America and remained active in the Dominican Republic, including participating in charitable activities, which earned him awards and honors there. In the United States, he served as president of the Council of Fashion Designers of America (CFDA) for many years and was given a Lifetime Achievement Award by the CFDA in 1990. De la Renta was also a patron of the arts. He served on many boards, including at Carnegie Hall and The Metropolitan Opera. Despite battling cancer during the last several years of his life, de la Renta remained active in the fashion world and was a sought-after designer.

8

⇝ ELIZABETH ARDEN ⇜

Hello, there! Thank you much for listening to the likes of me! I am Elizabeth Arden, and I am pleased to give you some tips about the fashion industry.

The fashion industry! What a glorious, glorious industry. For where else can you make a lot of dough, as you might say, while making a lot of people quite happy in the process? I do mention money right off, for that was my forte as Elizabeth. I could turn pennies into quarters and quarters into dollars, etc., as Elizabeth. And so, I did!

I am here with you today to speak of how you might go about making some cash, as they say, in the fashion industry—while enjoying every moment, of course!

First, I would like to get something out of the way, okay? I would like to get out of the way the idea that all in the fashion industry do prey on the insecurities of potential customers. Yes, this might be true in some instances, but I assure you that is generally not the case!

Those of us in the fashion industry—in the Light and on the Earth Plane—truly want to help people feel better and fabulous about themselves. That is truly our goal! So, do put aside the notion that to make money in fashion you must be duplicitous in some way. This truly is not the case! (And regarding the limited amount of people who are out for pure gain—why that is a commonality between all businesses, wouldn't you agree!?)

On to my message now. How to be successful in the fashion industry?

Truly, I tell you now that it takes being true to yourself—to your core self—to your core fundamentals. What do I mean by this? You know who you are. You know what makes you "tick," as they say. You also know what means a great deal to you in the fashion realm—be that clothing or accessories or handbags or hairstyles or makeup or divine perfume! When you tap into your fashion favorites, as I did in my life as Elizabeth, you truly can't help but soar in the business department of fashion!

Of course, you also need some commonsense. On one hand, this goes without saying, but on the other, it must be said! If you are the type that does struggle here and there with commonsense, I do wish to let you know that it is a muscle that you can most certainly strengthen. It is! Will it be harder for you than others? Why yes, it will be! But then again, there will be aspects that will be easier for you than for others— so it all "comes out in the wash," as they say!

Now that we've ascertained that you need to know you and what makes you tick and that you need some commonsense, what else shall I share with you? For I am already running out of room here! Let me enumerate a quick list!

1. There are always new horizons. Truly, keep this in mind. I urge you to avoid thinking of things as final and limited. If one line of perfume doesn't work or isn't snapped up by a company, there are plenty of options! For one, you can start your own line. The fashion world truly is your vibrant, lovely oyster!

2. Keep your hopes up—always. For the more hopeful you are, the more you believe, and the more you believe, the more "miracles" will come your way!

3. Watch your pennies, and the dollars will watch themselves. Truly! If you focus on the "little things" when it comes to your finances, the bigger things will work out in the end. Does this mean turning a blind eye to the bigger financial aspects? Of course not! But by focusing on the small things in finance, I assure you when you get to the big things you will be more than prepared to tackle those!

4. Use your senses to the fullest—and do protect their integrity. When you are developing a scent, inhale it to your tippy toes! Surround yourself with the scent for hours at a time. For that is the only way for you to know if something really, truly works! The same goes with clothing design. Do wrap yourself in your designs and live with them. Go about your days in them so that you will know if they are truly comfortable and elegant.

Also, protect your senses. Do take good care of your body, so that your eyes and nose and ears and mouth and hands do work as well as they can!

5. Do give back. When the money flows in, allow some of it to flow back out. For living in gratitude and giving and receiving will certainly make you the richest and wisest and most successful fashion industry mogul you can be! There is much to be said for giving. And that could very well be giving of fashion "goodies" to those in need.

I have most definitely shared enough for today! I do wish you a most glorious experience in the fashion industry. Do call on me if you wish for some tips. I am most happy to offer up my wisdom from here in the Light Plane Fashion Industry School of Thought and Development!

Good Day (or Evening) to You Always!
Yours,
Elizabeth Arden

—⊗⊗⊗—

FLORENCE NIGHTINGALE GRAHAM (Elizabeth Arden) was a Canadian-born American fashion industry businesswoman born on December 31, 1884. She died at the age of 81 on October 18, 1966. Arden is known for developing an internationally successful line of cosmetics, as well as a chain of beauty salons and spas. The beauty pioneer changed the face of cosmetics. Prior to Arden, cosmetics were considered low-class. She made their use acceptable among all women. Arden also pioneered the creation of the "beauty makeover." Born in Canada, the beauty mogul was the youngest of five children in a poor farming family. To help support the family, she worked as a youth and then studied to become a nurse. Her training included learning about lotions used in burn treatments, which fascinated Arden. She emigrated to New York City in 1908, where she began working as an assistant to a beautician. In 1910, she opened her first salon on Fifth Avenue with a partner. By 1915, her products were selling internationally. In 1922, Arden opened a salon in Paris, and in later years had salons across Europe and in Australia and South America. She also operated beauty spas. When she died, Arden had opened more than 100 salons worldwide and had created a line of about 300 cosmetic products. Arden was also a racehorse owner and suffragette. During her lifetime, she concealed her age, which wasn't revealed until her death. Arden did this to give the impression of timeless beauty.

—⊗⊗⊗—

"To be beautiful is the birthright of every woman."
—*Elizabeth Arden*

9

❧ RUSLANA KORSHUNOVA ❧

Привет. Hello, I am Ruslana Korshunova. And I am very happy to present here. Thank you for listening to me.

Beauty. What is beauty? Certainly, you know beauty when you see it. I was a rare beauty as Ruslana. By rare I mean that there were no others truly like me. And yet there were. That is the issue, shall I say now that I'm in the Light, of enticing and beguiling beauty. It does mesmerize you, and then it is quite ethereal and can quite literally disappear right before your eyes!

I don't mean to be a downer here. I only comment on beauty for beauty's sake. For truly, beauty is inside of us all, and beauty is more than looks. It is in the smile that one person gives to another, and it is in the actions of a beloved pet as he or she rushes to the door to see you. Yes, beauty is temporary on the outside and permanent on the inside.

Why am I speaking of this? I would like to tell you that if you are concerned about how you look, or how someone in your life looks, or you feel badly for someone else struggling with "image issues," that you needn't be. This isn't to say that people won't be troubled by their appearance. It's just to assure you that in the Light there are no outward appearances that matter. For beauty is in the vibration of an individual—each and every individual. I say this so that you know whenever you arrive here that you will be arriving as beautiful as the next person!

Okay, I have said my piece regarding this. What now? How about if you suspend your judgment the next time you look in the mirror? How about if you simply smile at your reflection? How about if you thank your body for getting you from point A to point B and for doing the best possible job while completing this mission?

How about if you give yourself and everyone you know and everyone you don't know, a break for being human and being themselves! How about if you embrace the idea that beauty is not just skin deep, but it is a very part of your very being.

I know this is all sounding a bit "out there," but I assure you, the answers are truly in you. They just are.

Does this mean I am suggesting that you not strive to be beautiful—to fulfill the standard of beauty on the Earth Plane now? No, I am not. For those of you reading this, if you feel so compelled, by all means strive for such a goal! For if you are meant to be a model—to model beauty in one or many of its form, then you are meant to do so.

Or perhaps you are meant to be a talent scout and find those beauties who can be models. That is a wonderful profession, as well. And quite exciting as you do look around for the next great model and find a gemstone hiding under a rock, so to speak! All I am meaning to say here is that beauty is beauty is beauty. Truly, beauty is around you every day, as I mentioned prior. It is in the everything of your existence. You need only look. And if you are meant to join the fashion industry, why then, how wonderful! I do wish you much joy and satisfaction with what is truly a noble profession!

And for those of you who are wondering about the "fashion machine" that has been said to spit out beauties once it has devoured them, I won't disagree with this entirely. For I was in a sense such a beauty as Ruslana. But I will remind you that humans do go to the Earth Plane to learn lessons—and to teach them. While I most certainly learned some lessons as Ruslana, I can tell you now that I truly was there to teach those watching my life as it was—as it turned out. So that others could be aware in the future. That is all I am privy to say currently about that!

I certainly don't want to leave this on a "sour" note!! So, please do embrace beauty wherever and however you do see it!! Do admire the beautiful models as they model the beautiful clothing and thank those who "found" them and brought them to the attention of the world. At the same time, do see the beauty in innocent things in life, like small children and puppies and kitties and butterflies and __ . You fill in the blank. Because yes, beauty truly is in the eye of the beholder!! It just is!

That's all for me today! I wish you a blessed time on the Earth Plane.

Good Day to You Always,
Ruslana Korshunova

RUSLANA SERGEYEVNA KORSHUNOVA (Руслана Сергеевна Коршунова) was a Kazakh model of Russian descent born on July 2, 1987. She died at the age of 20, due to falling from a ninth-floor window in an action ruled suicide, on June 28, 2008. Nicknamed the Russian Rapunzel, Korshunova captured the attention of the fashion world with her stunning beauty, which included knee-length blonde hair and riveting deep gray eyes. She appeared in magazines such as *Vogue* and the French *Elle* and modeled for designers such as Vera Wang. Korshunova was born in the former Republic of Kazakhstan, the last republic to leave the USSR on December 16, 1991. Her father died when she was five years old. Korshunova was discovered in 2003 by a model scout, who saw her photo in an article about a German language club. Korshunova spoke Russian, Kazakh, German, and English. She also modeled in print ads for various designers and brands, including Nina Ricci, Clarins, Max Studio, and Pantene Always Smooth. After her death, it was discovered that she'd had a relationship with an older wealthy man, who had cast her aside.

She also became involved in a Moscow-based organization that some have called a cult. Korshunova was buried at Khovanskoye Cemetery in Moscow, one of her favorite cities.

10

❥ ÉTIENNE AIGNER ❦

Hello there! Étienne Aigner here. Most pleased to present!

Well, how do you do? Truly, how do you do? For how you do is tied into what I would like to say here. It truly is! For how you do is what your clothing and accessories do say about you. By this I don't mean how much money you have. Rather, I am talking about how the clothes on your back and the bag on your arm do say a lot about you from the very outset.

When one meets another, truly, the clothing is what one does look at first. Wouldn't you agree? And then the divine accessories, such as the shoes and the jewelry and the handbag, of course, as was one of my specialties as Etienne!

Let us discuss handbags. For they are quite utterly, deliciously divine in their very own right. How a woman (or man, if he so chooses) holds a handbag does say so much. For having a bag flung over your shoulder communicates something entirely different than clutching a bag in your hand or under your arm. And then, of course, not having a handbag does say quite a bit as well. But that is another matter—however, not! For the minimalistic look is truly a fashion statement as well.

But let us return to the handbag. The divine, sweet, lovely handbag! Oh, how rapturous, really, is the handbag in its most pristine form. The thrill of getting a new handbag! If it is leather, smelling the leather

40

of the handbag. Inhaling it deeply and swooning at the delicious fragrance of the bag! I know I do wax on. But as mentioned, handbags (and leather) were my specialty in my lifetime as Étienne. And those of you who have gotten a new handbag do know what I mean about the rapture you will most likely feel looking at the bag in its most pristine form!

The thrill of what you can put in the bag. The compartments. I did so love to design bags with various compartments—in fact, secret compartments, even. For what is more thrilling than seeing the handbag empty is seeing the handbag full—overflowing with all of those "necessities" that women and men do find it necessary to stuff into their bags. Never mind if only a mere fraction of those items are used on a regular basis. The fact that you have this divine handbag with all these items does give one a bit of security, wouldn't you agree? For it is a lot like taking the kitchen sink with you at times—especially when you have a rather large, "luggage style" bag! Dear Julie does have these quite cute bags made for her that are tiny in comparison to the luggage style bags—and yet they have a life of their own. Truly, they do sparkle and shine with their tininess! And she manages to fit quite a lot in them!

What of the colors of the handbags? I did so adore doing market research and thinking and pondering about the colors to use for handbags. For color is such a powerful thing, as they say. Color does put you in a certain mood. Not to mention that the colors of one's handbags does make a big difference when one is color coordinating one's wardrobe and persona!

Oh, colors, colors, colors! Bright colors are so bright, and so bold, and so exciting! And certainly, they can be used to excess at times, but then that is okay. For how divine to have a bright turquoise handbag to go with a turquoise necklace—all blended with a magnificent white outfit, or even yellow!! Colors, I so love you! Yes, I know, I am getting overexcited, but truly that is quite impossible here!! Another matter, of course. I only say this because I am so thrilled to present here. And the fact that Julie did agree to play some Stravinsky as I wrote this. He is one of my favorites, and he does make one feel hyperexcited about everything!! (He is in book #3 of the Channeled Masters series, for those of you interested in music.)

At any rate, I do hope you enjoyed my "rant," if you will, on the beauty and form and utterly divine function of the purse. For what woman can go without a purse? It is difficult to leave the house without one, wouldn't you say? Where to put all your stuff? (I know, I know! There are some of you able to do this—however, this isn't for you!! Not to be rude or anything, ha ha!) But purses for most women—and some men—are truly a necessity. So why not have the most magnificent, utterly divine purses that you can possibly have!!

That is all for me now. I could go on for several more pages about purses, but I think you "get my drift," as you say in your day!!

Ta ta to you! And thank you ever so much for reading. I am deeply honored.

Yours,

Étienne Aigner

———∞———

ÉTIENNE AIGNER was a Hungarian-born fashion designer born on November 8, 1904. He died at the age of 95 on November 5, 2000. Aigner is best known for developing the high fashion houses, Étienne Aigner, based in New York City and Munich, Germany. Both companies specialize in luxury goods, including handbags, wallets, leather accessories, shoes, and women's apparel. Aigner is known for creating timeless signature designs that are also functional, which quickly became popular amongst American women when he opened his first showroom in 1959 in New York City. He soon became known as "The Man With the Golden Hands" for his superior craftsmanship and willingness to embrace modern designs and techniques. He is considered responsible for the preppy look of the 1960s and 1970s. Aigner was born in Ersekujvar, Hungary. He began working with leather while still a teenager and became a bookbinder to make money. In the 1930s, he and his older brother moved to Paris, where he continued to bind books until World War II began. Aigner had converted from Judaism to Catholicism when he married a Frenchwoman, but still found himself in danger. For protection, he joined a group of Resistance Fighters in the Massif Central region of France. After the war ended, he returned to Paris and began making handbags and belts. He soon attracted the notice of major fashion houses like Dior (#33). In 1950, he moved to New York and tried working for a mass production handbag manufacturer, but this didn't suit him well. Soon, he struck out on his own. Aigner began making belts in his bedroom. He found it economical to stick to a deep red that became his signature. Within a few years, he had belts and handbags at high-end department stores throughout the country. He sold his part of the company in 1967. By that time, they were also offering classic pumps and other accessories. Aigner created his own logo, which is still found on the brand's products. He used the A in his last name shaped into a horseshoe, creating an omega symbol.

11

❧ GUCCIO GUCCI ❧

Hello, and ciao, I am Guccio Gucci. And I am honored to present here in this most fabulous work—full of fabulous fashion tips. Begin, we shall.

Oh, the glorious handbag!! Truly, it is such a beloved accessory. For quite a lot of reasons, but then my friend Étienne did cover this quite extraordinarily. I shall add to the "fray" as they say, as well, when it comes to handbags and other leather goods.

Leather!! What a divine material!! It is so durable and enduring and classically good looking, no matter what its age and no matter in what manner it is used. Leather is divine, and leather is absolutely gorgeous when it is processed and treated well and fashioned into lovely accessories like belts and gloves and handbags, and shoes, of course!!

What shall I say about shoes? For shoes are most glorious, in so many ways. Shoes do get you from point A to point Z, and shoes do get you there in a fashionable and comfortable way—if you choose the ideal shoes for you! I did love shoes as Gucci, as well. For designing them and watching them be walked around in was a glorious experience! I shall tell you!

What else about shoes? Well, there is much, I'm sure you would agree! For there is a form and function that occurs with shoes. Shoes must look elegant and lovely or sporty and casual, or whatever it is you are striving to attain by way of looks, and then shoes must also be as

44

comfortable as possible. And then shoes must also do a good job of "showing off" a person's leg and attire. Certainly, this is something that is quite evident in a pump when a woman does wear the pump with a skirt or dress. Of course, men's shoes add to the entire effect of the person's attire. Shoes can certainly "make" a man, as they say, while shoes do adorn a woman!

Am I digressing about shoes? Well, of course I am! For that was my right and prerogative as Gucci. It can be your right and prerogative, as well, if you choose to take the journey as a designer.

Of course, my life as Gucci—my career path—was quite different than is likely to occur for you today. However, there are some precepts, shall we say, that remain set in stone when it comes to becoming and being a designer. They are enduring tips, throughout the ages. I shall number them for you here, to help you decide if you wish to be a designer, and then to design with abandon and "hit it big." If you choose, of course—for this is all free will. Every last bit of it!!

1) Get a proper education. Yes, you heard that right! Get educated in the fashion design realm, however you see fit to do so. This will give you the basics so that you can one day run with your own designs, built on the strong foundation of the basics! This is of critical importance—starting with the basics and building on them. Much like a building needs a strong foundation, so does your designing career.

2) Figure out if you truly wish to be a designer. Not everyone is "made" for designing. By getting a bit of an education on the topic and watching other designers work and reading their bios, etc., you will soon enough determine if you would like to be a designer, after all.

3) Keep an open mind. There are so many tastes in the world and so many ideas of what represents "high" fashion and low fashion, even. Rather than walking around with preconceived notions, keep your heart and mind open to all. This will help you design your best work, and design work that resonates with a wide audience—which is of critical importance!

4) At the same time, do hold your fashion convictions close to your chest. You will have certain beliefs as to what makes "good" fashion, and that is rather divine! For those beliefs will become your signature style—what makes your work shine through and out to the world. So, do hold tight to those items that you feel strongly about. Just keep in mind that this will only work if there are a few precepts to which you hold tight. This does not work well if you hold tight to a smorgasbord of beliefs.

5) Keep a positive mindset about your designs and the design life. I know many say this, but that is because this bears repeating. It is simply a must to stay positive, for that will ensure that you stay focused on your goals and that you continue with the belief to your very being that you will succeed—because you will with that attitude!

6) Align yourself with likeminded souls. This means designers, as well as seamstresses and models and those who study the fashion industry and write about it. And of course, fans of your work who wish to wear your designs and model them for all the world to see! There is much to be said for the power of good, strong community that lifts you up always!

7) Know. Know that you are on your exact right path, even if that path has taken you to removing the creases from slacks in a design or rethinking the name of your line, or….you get the picture. This is all a process. And you are on the road of that magnificent process that will take you to fabulous fashion always!

*Good day to you. I've taken up quite a bit of space, so I shall say
ciao now. See you in the Light Plane Fashion School!*
    Yours,
    Gucci

———— ⌘ ————

GUCCIO GUCCI was an Italian fashion designer and businessman born
on March 26, 1881. He died at the age of 71, due to natural causes, on
January 2, 1953. Gucci is the founder of the famed Italian luxury
brand of fashion and leather goods known as Gucci. He founded the
company in Florence, Italy in 1921, initially specializing in leather
goods. In the 1930s, he became inspired by horse racing and began
designing hardware for his leather goods that resembled various horse-
related items, like bits and stirrups. He created the loafer shoe in 1932
with a gilded snaffle (most common type of bit used for horses). In
1947, he introduced the Bamboo handbag, a saddlebag featuring
bamboo handles that is still produced today. Gucci's father was a
leather goods maker. When Gucci was a porter at the Savoy hotel in
London as a teen, he became inspired by how the well-off clients
dressed and by their luggage. The House of Gucci originally started as a
family-owned leather saddlery shop but expanded from there to later
include high-fashion. Gucci had six children with his wife, Aida
Calvelli. His four sons took active, prominent roles in the company. In
1953, the company expanded overseas to New York, not long after his
death.

12

✤ KARL LAGERFELD ✤

Hello, Karl Lagerfeld here! Delighted to present. I daresay I almost didn't make it into this book, being that I only recently left the Earth Plane! But that is as ordained, as is all of this.

Ordained. What is ordained? Certainly, your interest in fashion is ordained, if you are a "clothes horse," as they say, or a fashion diva, or a designer, or wish to be one. Certainly, I was a fashion designer as Karl, among many other interests I had! And a very full life I did live as Karl.

What shall we discuss today? Fashion, of course. Delightful fashion. For as I mentioned, those of you interested in fashion most certainly have always been so. In prior lifetimes, even. For fashion is an incredible occupation and pastime. Of that you can be sure!

What else shall I tell you?

Well, how about this? How about if you do suspend belief for a bit and try a little "exercise," if you will? What if you could see yourself through the ages enjoying fashion? Perhaps you have been a tailor in a lifetime, and a cobbler in another, and a jewelry maker in another, like my dear friend Miriam Haskell (#13)? In another life you designed magnificent ballgowns, while in another you were a seamstress to royalty!

What would you do with all this information if you had it at your disposal? Most certainly, a lot of what you like in this lifetime would soon make sense, as would your proclivity towards fashion in all its beauty. At the same time, would knowing that you succeeded with fashion in prior lifetimes give you the good "kick in the pants" necessary to know that you can take advantage of those skills in this lifetime and make a name for yourself in fashion?

That could most certainly happen, couldn't it?

Did I know that I had prior lifetimes (many) in the fashion realm when I was walking amongst you as Karl? Perhaps. I can tell you for sure that I did know that I had a driving, deep desire to pursue all things fashion and to share the beauty and the enchantment and the utter Earthly divinity of fashion in all its guises. That did propel me. I knew that I wouldn't be sustained or fulfilled if I didn't surround myself with fashion and make it my life's work.

Does this sound like something that resonates with you? This knowing that fashion is indeed a part of you and that you most certainly won't live a complete life if you don't surround yourself with the beauty and excitement and pure, unadulterated thrill of fashion? If that is the case, I do urge you, if you haven't done so already, to pursue a life of fashion in whatever means it shall fit in your life. That could mean that you do surround yourself with fashionable clothing—and adorn yourself as well. It could also mean that you become a seamstress to the stars or that you design fabulous women's or menswear for oodles of people. It could also mean that you create divine jewelry or purses or belts or shoes. Or that you create and run a fashion empire, as did yours truly and many others in this book. Or that you focus on the utter beauty and charming nature of the female head of hair.

Whatever you do in the fashion realm, see that it resonates with your soul! If that is the case, you truly can never go wrong. For it is your soul that you do take back here to the Light, and it is your soul that you drag about with you always. You do need to leave your fashions—your clothing and accessories—behind. But then you can leave them behind for others to enjoy. And your designs can truly continue for eternity when passed down in the right hands!

That is all from me now. I do have a "photo shoot" of sorts to do here regarding a fashion spread that we are concocting to share with fashion trendsetters on Earth in the right time and space! Good Day to you always. I do wish you a lifetime of enjoying fashion in its many beatific forms.

    Yours Truly,

    Karl Lagerfeld

KARL OTTO LAGERFELD was a German fashion designer, creative director, photographer, artist, and caricaturist born on September 10, 1933. He died at the age of 85, due to complications of pancreatic cancer, on February 19, 2019. Lagerfeld was known for his position as creative director of Chanel in Paris. He was also creative director of Fendi, known for its Italian furs and leather goods, and of his own fashion label. Lagerfeld had his own signature, widely recognized look that consisted of white hair, fingerless gloves, black sunglasses and high, starched collars. Lagerfeld was born in Hamburg. His father owned a company that imported evaporated milk. When his mother met his father, she was selling lingerie. As a child, Lagerfeld showed interest in the visual arts. Schoolmates said he was always sketching. Outspoken, Lagerfeld said he only continued to attend school in Germany to learn the French language, so he could move there, which he did, living much of his life in Paris. In 1955, he began his career as an assistant to French fashion designer Pierre Balmain. Lagerfeld joined Chanel in 1983, spending the next 36 years there, taking the company from a small fashion house to an industry leader. He also lent his design sense to Fendi. Bernard Arnault, the chairman and chief executive of LVMH, which owns Fendi, said that Lagerfeld was "a creative genius who helped make Paris the fashion capital of the world and Fendi one of the most innovative Italian houses." Arnault also called Lagerfeld immensely imaginative. German model Claudia Schiffer said of Lagerfeld: "Karl was my magic dust, he transformed me from a shy German girl into a supermodel...what Warhol was to art, he was to fashion; he is irreplaceable." Lagerfeld also had a celebrity pet—his cat Choupette.

⸻

"Sweatpants are a sign of defeat. You lost control of your life, so you bought some sweatpants."
—*Karl Lagerfeld*

13

≫ MIRIAM HASKELL ≪

*Hello, and greetings! Miriam Haskell here! Come to talk fashion
and primarily costume jewelry! Thank you for "having me."*

My, how grand is the fashion world and pursuit of fashion! I did
so love fashion as Miriam. Most specifically, I loved costume
jewelry! That was such a delightful occupation! I must tell you, I did
love the fact that the jewelry I made, though it does sell for quite a bit
today, was not a precious commodity back then. I did prefer, I must
say, to not have to worry about the cut of a dear, precious diamond.
Afterall, beads and materials such as cubic zirconia are so much easier
to meld and deal with!

That being said, I would like to comment on the fact that there is
truly nothing "more precious" than anything else here. At the same
time, what is precious to you may not be precious to another. That was
another thing I so adored about "costume" jewelry. You could make an
item precious just by falling in love with it!

What shall I tell you about costume jewelry? Well, certainly, it is a
fashion statement in its own right. Costume jewelry does have a bit or
a lot of pizzazz to it! It surely does! And it can be used to dress up just
about any outfit. For truly, where else can you find the wide range of
colors and color tones, than in costume jewelry?

And the character that can be imbued into a piece of costume jewelry! Oh, my. The designer can quite literally put his or her mark on

the jewelry—brand it into the jewelry, in fact, so that it becomes a very part of the piece! That is something that can be done with items that are a bit malleable, shall we say.

What else?

How about this? What if you were to think of your own fashion ideas as pieces of costume jewelry? What if you gave yourself the latitude and longitude, shall we say, to create whatever you wish, knowing that it is likely to appeal to people—often many people— despite its "cheaper" costume cost? What would you do? Would you design with abandon, unaware and unconcerned about what is considered costume and what is considered precious and "real?" I bet you would!

What shall I tell you about designing costume jewelry? First, I would like to suggest that you do make your molds very strongly, so that they can stand up to the test of time and the test of manufacturing. At the same time, I do suggest that you make a limited amount of one piece, and that you do then break the mold, literally. For if you want your costume jewelry to gain a bit or a lot of "status," you do want to have "limited edition" pieces. Of course, you can hide the mold in case you find that a piece would do well to come "back." Just don't tell anyone this—or where it is located!

I know this may sound a bit cloak and dagger, but I assure you that is what good marketing is made of. I will end my selection with a few tidbits for you to savor about selling products. Hopefully these "pointers" will assist you!

1. Love what you are making and selling. This is an absolute MUST! Truly, you can't sell well those things that you just don't have your heart into. You just can't!

2. Access all that comes to you—but be judicious in what you choose. Once you begin creating in the fashion world, ideas will begin to come flying at you, much like gnats to the window shield of a moving car. Your job, if you choose to take it, is to ensure that all that you decide to take on, as they say, is to your liking. Truly, what you are working on really should make your heart sing. This includes marketing ideas for your products. (Of course, you must work to live at times—and that is a different matter altogether.)

3. Know that what you do create is utterly divine, and many will desire your creations. In more ways than one! You are the "keeper," shall we say, of the most divine of creations. Right there in your noggin'! Do know that you have in you the most magnificent designs, if you choose to access them.

4. Know also that we will be there to help you—should you ask for help. We fashion designers and models here in the Light are standing at attention with pencil and pattern and needle and thread and scissors (if we're "talking" hair) in hand! We shall come "flying" to help you—quite literally! And we have quite grand marketing ideas!

5. Every list I feel should have a 5! Believe in yourself and your dreams. Just do so! For that is the beginning, middle and the end—truly! When you believe, do watch out! For that is when the magic happens and dreams do come true! Your sales will and can quite literally shoot through the roof!

> *Good day to you! I am honored to have presented here to share my "bit" about costume jewelry and the very essence of being a fashion designer—guru, even. Fashion fun to you always!*
> *Yours,*
> *Miriam Haskell*

MIRIAM HASKELL was an American jewelry designer, who pioneered costume jewelry. She died at the age of 82 on July 14, 1981. Haskell is noted for her colorful, eye-catching, and affordable costume jewelry pieces. She created her handmade pieces from the 1920s through the 1960s, which included periods of economic hardship, such as the Great Depression and the war years. Haskell began designing jewelry around the same time as Coco Chanel (#6) launched a *faux* jewelry line. Haskell's jewelry also competed with that of Italian designer Elsa Schiaparelli (#14). Haskell designed the jewelry with her creative partner, Frank Hess, who she met when he was a window dresser for Macy's. Haskell used her strong business acumen to build the company (Haskell Jewels) that still exists today, as well as collaborated with Hess on the jewelry design. She began by opening shops in New York City, where the company is still based. By the 1930s, Haskell had well-known women as her customers, including designer Gloria Vanderbilt (#20), and actresses such as Lucille Ball and Joan Crawford. Crawford was a particularly avid collector of Haskell's jewelry. Haskell was also a friend of Coco Chanel's (#6) and created pieces for her couture collections. Haskell's jewelry was known for quality, exquisite detail, and workmanship. After design, each piece went to the workshop of craftsmen—many of whom were European refugees familiar with the jewelry trade. They would wire complex, multi-layered motifs, using tight embroidery and superior wiring that resulted in high-quality, distinctive pieces. Depending on the economic climate, Haskell used a wide variety of materials for her jewelry. For instance, when European bead supplies were limited during World War II, she had Hess create metal-free jewelry designs with plastics and natural materials sourced close to home. After the war, Haskell went back to using higher-end materials, such as pearls from Japan. Today, Haskell's jewelry pieces are collector's items.

14

❧ ELSA SCHIAPARELLI ❧

Hello! I am Elsa Schiaparelli. I am honored to present. Truly!
Thank you so much for "visiting—and listening!"

Fashion, fashion, fashion!! High fashion, "low" fashion, even. Just fashion! For that is what I ate and drank and slept as Elsa! I so did!

What shall I tell you about fashion? Well, I would like to share what I do believe are the key elements of becoming involved in a fashion industry existence, shall we say. And then I would also like to talk to you about your own personal fashion sense.

Let's begin with working in the fashion industry. Of course, when I lived the life of Elsa, I was quite a bit ahead of my time, so to speak. For there were very few women in fashion—save for darlings like my dear friend Coco (#6). (Yes, we were archrivals on the Earth Plane. A funny little twist we put into our life scripts, for we are "very tight," as they say, here!) Truly, there were very few of us. Most certainly less than the fingers on one hand!

Today, of course, there are many women in the fashion field in various capacities. And many women who made great, deep marks in the industry, whom you can study. But back then, it was quite difficult.

Does that mean that you don't now have difficulties? Of course, you do! Even along the male-female lines in business. But I am not here to discuss that particularly. What I would like to discuss, however, or should I say suggest, is that you do take a good look at the women in history who made inroads that you can now travel. People like me, of course, and Coco, and Elizabeth Arden (#8). And many more!

Why am I suggesting that you look to us to see what we did? Well, for one, I do suggest this so that you can gain inspiration and valuable know-how. For we were truly inspiring in those lifetimes, and we did know what we were doing. At least most of the time!

What did we know back then that would help you in the here and now? Well, for one, we did know that we would succeed. We just knew it. You may have been urged to internalize this, and yet you haven't yet. I do urge you to internalize this—if nothing else. YOU WILL SUCCEED—providing you wish to! Will you succeed on the first attempt? Maybe, but maybe not. The second iteration or alteration? Maybe, but maybe not. Will the third time be a charm, as they say? Quite possibly. The point is not to ask when, just to know that it will happen, and just to forge on. Period! That is all there is to it!!

So, do forge on with your designs, and your ideas, and your enthusiasm for fashion. All of this will help you achieve your dreams—to vast proportions!

What else will looking at the work of the fashion greats do for you? It will spur more ideas. It will make you jump from their ideas to your own ideas. Seeing that their ideas came to fruition will most certainly ensure that your ideas do the same.

The fashion greats will also teach you that fashion truly is an "art form" that has and will always stand the test of time. You will always be introduced to beautiful fashion forms and fashion sense by those in the fashion industry—including yourself. It is just something that will truly always be!

I did say I would say a few words about your own fashion sense. And so, I shall. How do you feel about your own fashion sense? Truly feel? Do you become excited about how you present yourself through fashion? Or do you feel a bit lost or a bit stymied or stunted, even? I ask this, because I assure you that there are solutions to every fashion dilemma. There certainly are!

What shall you do if you feel as if you aren't as pizzazzy, shall we say, as possible?

Ask yourself this question, and then do grab hold of the very first thing that comes to mind.

What is it you truly wish to wear? Did you picture yourself in a hat? Did you picture yourself with red or even green hair? Did you picture yourself with flowing scarves wrapped around your head? Whatever you saw is a direct line to your fashion cravings, shall we say. Once you begin to satisfy your fashion cravings, Dear Fashion Masters in Training, you will most certainly alight on the keys to your fashion kingdom. Then watch out! For you will find your own personal fashion sensing soaring. That will most certainly spill into any work you should choose to do in the blessed, absolutely forever fabulous Fashion Industry!

Good day to you. And thank you once again for listening to the "likes" of me!
  Yours,
  Elsa Schiaparelli

ELSA SCHIAPARELLI was an Italian fashion designer born on September 10, 1890. She died at the age of 83 in her sleep on November 13, 1973. Schiaparelli is known for having brought a certain shock factor into the fashion industry. Her designs were influenced by surrealism and often considered irreverent. She was the first couturier to point out the amusing side of fashion. This brought her notoriety and attention from artists, including Salvador Dali, with whom she collaborated. Notable fashion designs she and the artist created that caused a stir include the "Skeleton Dress," created for her Circus Collection. It was a black crepe dress with quilting that represented a spine, leg bones, and ribs. Schiaparelli also designed costumes for several films. She was born to an aristocrat mother and scholar father. She studied philosophy at the University of Rome, where she published a book of sensual poetry that was considered scandalous. This caused her parents to put her in a convent. However, Schiaparelli went on a hunger strike and was released from the convent. She then became a nanny in London where she met her husband, Count William de Wendt de Kerlor. They moved to New York, and she had a daughter. When her marriage failed due to her husband's infidelity, Schiaparelli moved to Paris and began to design and make clothing, starting her own business in 1927. She mixed with and dressed many famous people at the time, including Greta Garbo, Mae West, and Jean Cocteau. Schiaparelli's famous perfume, Shocking, was inspired after the designer went to Hollywood and met West. The perfume became an instant success, as well as the dress based on the perfume that contained air pockets in the bodice that could be blown up to create the well-known Mae West bosom. Schiaparelli's designs included other firsts, such as visible zippers in clothing. The zippers, as well as unusual buttons, became key signatures of her work. Some of the items represented on her unusual buttons included ships, crickets, candlesticks, and even silk-covered carrots and cauliflowers. Schiaparelli was one of the first people in fashion to recognize the work of future Tiffany & Co. jewelry designer, Jean Schlumberger, who designed buttons for her.

15

✦ VIDAL SASSOON ✦

*Hello! Most honored and feeling privileged to present! I am Vidal
Sassoon, and I am here to talk about hair, glorious, absolutely fabulous hair, hair, hair!!*

Oh, my, how absolutely, positively beautiful and delightful is the
human head of hair! We do have a sort of hair here—but is it
much less tangible here in the Light. Certainly, hair on the Earth is
quite glorious to behold! A lovely hairdo, a lovely tousled "mess" of
hair, even. There is truly no other "part" of the body as glorious as
absolutely fabulous hair!

Okay, so I have gotten that out of the way, as they say. My utterly
divine love of hair—fascination with the truly glorious substance!! Let
me give you something that you can use about hair, as one who is
interested in the glorious fashion realm!

The health of your hair. Truly, the health of your hair does matter
very much! How does one get a flowing, full, thick mane of fabulous
hair! Truly, that question is asked quite a bit on the Earth Plane, I think
you will agree! And while heredity does play a part, there are some
things you can do to help your hair stay as healthy as possible.

Julie does have a fabulous head of glorious hair! She truly does. And
while heredity does play a part—she can thank her German great
grandmother with her long mane of hair still intact in her 90s—Julie
does some things that do help her hair stay healthy and buoyant.

Here is my prescription for a lovely, healthy mane of hair. This does apply to you guys, as well!

1. Nutrition. Yes, what you eat certainly affects your lovely strands of hair. It just does! There truly is no getting around this. While you needn't keep a rigid, structured diet that would put one to sleep just thinking about it—there are certain items that should be included in a good diet to help your hair along, shall we say. And then there are those items to not overdo, including alcohol and nitrates.

But what are the "good" items to include? It is quite simple, actually! Lots of Veggies and Fruits!! I capitalize them, because I wish to emphasize their utmost importance. They are full of vitamins that will give you a healthy head of hair. And while you can certainly get vitamins from other sources, the vitamins in vegetables are readily absorbed by your hair follicles. They just are! It is Mother Nature's way of giving your hair immediate "love," shall we say.

2. Water. I didn't include this in the prior point, because it is of importance to emphasize this all on its own! Water, water, water! Do drink your water. For water gives your hair the buoyancy you do so crave, and water helps transport those vitamins from the veggies and fruits (and minerals) into your hair follicles—I assure you. If you don't "like" water, I can only say pooh, pooh to you! For water is an elixir. Change your thinking, if you can, about drinking water!

3. Hair Care. Your haircare regimen—it most likely won't surprise you—does have a big effect on the health of your hair! Regular washing, but with shampoos and conditioners and treatment agents that aren't harsh. Make it as mild as possible! And do spend some money on your hair products. Those you can find at your favorite salon are often high-quality and worth every penny. I assure you!

4. Blow Drying. I do realize that there are certain styles that require a nice, hot stream of air so you can do what you wish to do with your do, so to speak! But when possible, do let your hair dry naturally. If you must dry at all, just dry the scalp and let your tresses air-dry from there! And when possible, do use a cool or semi-warm stream of air when styling with the blow drier.

5. Brushing. If you are concerned about your hair. If it is brittle or slow growing, which can happen from certain health conditions and the resulting medications, as well, I do urge you to not brush your hair with a heavy hand and to avoid brushing as much as possible. I know this goes contrary to the 100 brushes a day, but truly it is best to avoid the brush when there are problems with your hair. You can run your fingers through your hair to untangle, and then do brush a bit.

6. Be Kind to Yourself and Your Hair. I mentioned health conditions and resulting medications that can affect the health of your hair. These are very real reasons for hair to experience trouble, shall we say. While it will most certainly help to address the underlying illness/disease that does cause the hair loss or frailty, at the same time be kind to yourself and your hair. For truly, worrying about the state of your hair and being angry at yourself and your hair will make it have more troubles. The negative energy will do that. It just will!

7. Get Yourself a Great Hairstylist. Hairstylists are true hair artists! They are. They can help your hair look as good as it possibly can. And they can help your hair thrive, even, with their magical fingers. You will know you've found a great stylist when you feel absolutely lovely after he or she is done with your hair. And such a stylist will treat your glorious hair like gold! Because it is!!

That is all from me for now. I must get back to class in the Light Plane Fashion Institute's "Hair Salon Incubator." That is all I can say about that. I will see you when you pass, however, most likely in one of my classes. Or I shall be in one of your classes!! Good hair and good day or night to you always!

Yours Truly, Truly,

Vidal Sassoon

———— ❧ ————

VIDAL SASSOON was a British hairstylist and entrepreneur born on January 17, 1928. He died at the age of 84, due to leukemia, on May 9, 2012. Sassoon is best known for revolutionizing women's hairstyling in the 1950s and 1960s. He re-introduced the iconic bob hairstyle worn by movie stars such as Goldie Hawn and Mia Farrow. The wash-and-wear style went up against the then-prevalent bouffant sprayed and teased style. Sassoon had a lifelong interest in architecture, which came out in his hair designs that emphasized the use of precise scissor cuts and geometric angles. He strove to create simple styles that accented women's facial structures and hair textures. Sassoon had a difficult childhood. His father abandoned the family when he was young, which resulted in his spending part of his childhood in a Jewish orphanage. He was able to leave the orphanage when his mother remarried and got him an apprenticeship at a London barbershop. In 1954, he opened his own salon. By the mid-1960s, Sassoon was cutting the hair of celebrities. His career skyrocketed in 1968 when he created the ultra-short pixie cut for Mia Farrow when she starred in the movie classic, *Rosemary's Baby*. Sassoon went on to open salons and hairdressing schools throughout Europe and North America. He also co-founded Paul Mitchell Systems with Paul Mitchell (#19), once a student of his. Sassoon marketed his hair care products with the slogan: "If you don't look good, we don't look good." He sold his company in the early 1980s but continued to represent the brand. Sassoon went on to become a social activist and philanthropist. A documentary of his life released in 2010.

———⊗⊗⊗———

"The only place where success comes before work is in the dictionary."

"I was all about my thoughts, my work, my inspiration. I was always in hair."
    —*Vidal Sassoon*

16

❧ Jeanne Lanvin ❧

Hello! Jeanne Lanvin here. Pleased to present. Let us begin.

The beginning. What a grand "thing" is the beginning. The beginning of a design—the inklings and little snippets that I did see when I tapped in and began to "download" a design. That was a most exciting, ultra-thrilling time! For I so loved what I did as Jeanne. Designing, designing, designing! And for women. The female form is a most glorious form to design for!

Are there rules? Are there rules to fashion design? Most certainly there are. And yet, there is one "big" rule, shall we say, and that is to let go of all the rules. Refrain from allowing them to constrain you. However, this is AFTER you have learned the rules.

You no doubt have heard this before. Do learn the rules so that you can break the rules. Do tighten a bodice or keep a certain length to a hem so that you can loosen the bodice or lengthen—or even shorten—the hem.

Is this good, sound fashion advice? I think so! For the foundations are critical to learn and internalize and use. And then when you have that down pat, as they say, you can go ahead and break the rules—yet you will still have your strong foundation on which to pin those rules. That way while your hem may go up or down, the foundation of your garment remains impenetrable and does ensure that the model is well covered, shall we say.

Okay, I can hear you thinking! What is it that Jeanne wishes to truly say?

I shall say it.

In time.

That is another of my messages. In time.

Truly there is time for your fashion designs. Do give them time, and do know that they will appear in their exact right Divine time. They will! That means that if you are fretting over a design that simply won't "work," it isn't time for the design to spring forth. That is why the Universe, or us Fashion Masters, are keeping you from seeing the design come to full fruition—until it is time.

What else?

How about giving yourself a quarter every time you access a most divine thought about a divine design? You will soon find your pockets are jangling. I say this because those in the fashion world often think that they come up with very little. No doubt this is true of other creative pursuits. The fact is that your mind—your Divine Fashion Mind—is quite literally whirring like a sewing machine motor at all times! You need only acknowledge this fact, and then you shall begin to note all these grand designs.

What happens when you do this? You shall be compelled to draw a design on paper or computer—or even sit down at the sewing machine and put your prototype together!! It most certainly will happen if you do acknowledge all the grand designs that you come up with on a moment-by-moment basis.

What else?

How about this? How about if you do "measure" your success as well. As you might measure the inseam of a pair of pants. Do measure your successes in such an accurate and precise manner. You will find that your fashion successes are quite literally "the bomb," as I've heard you say in your day. But this can only happen if you do look to what you've created and how wondrous it is, and then do clap yourself on the back—or clap your hands for yourself.

And then, of course, do move on to the next task at hand!

Good day to you. I do hope that this helps you with your glorious Fashion Journey. I shall see you in the Light Plane Fashion School!
Yours Truly Forever and Ever,
Jeanne Lanvin

———————————— ❧ ————————————

JEANNE-MARIE LANVIN was a French designer born on January 1, 1867. She died at the age of 79 on July 6, 1946. Lanvin was one of the earliest female fashion entrepreneurs. She created supremely feminine clothing and had a passion for color—particularly blue. Lanvin initially worked as an apprentice milliner in her late teens and early twenties in Paris. From the beginning, she showed superior workmanship with her hat-making abilities. During this time, Lanvin became inspired to one day own her own fashion house. She did just that in 1893 and soon found success. Lanvin, who came from a family of 11 children, had her daughter, Marguerite, in 1897. Rather than slow her down, motherhood inspired Lanvin. Marguerite became her muse. Lanvin used luxurious fabrics, including delicate silks and intricate embroidery, to design Marguerite's elegant clothing. Soon mothers and daughters flocked to Lanvin's store. This prompted the fashion entrepreneur to open a children's clothing department in 1908. By 1909, Lanvin was selling more children's clothing than hats. Mothers and daughters went to her shop to get matching outfits. That same year Lanvin changed her status from milliner to fashion designer by becoming a member of the Parisian Fashion Council. Forever the visionary and a shrewd businesswoman, Lanvin continued to expand her fashion empire. She also touched elbows with artists, writers, and musicians of her time. This led to her dressing writer Louise de Vilmorin and silent movie star Mary Pickford. The work of those in the arts also inspired her designs and offerings. She met renowned architect and decorator Armand-

Albert Rateau, and the two created a store that carried interior design pieces, including curtains, stained glass, wallpaper, curtains, and rugs in Art Deco style common during that time. Lanvin also eventually expanded into lingerie, swimwear, fragrance, and menswear.

17

⇝ AUDREY HEPBURN ⇜

Hello! I am Audrey Hepburn. And I am quite pleased to speak of fashion. Like dear Marilyn, there was some talk about whether I should appear here or in the actors and actresses' book, but my fashion sense, shall we say, in my lifetime as Audrey landed me here! Hooray!

Fashion sense. Do you have a fashion sense? Have you just loved fashion since you can remember? Was dress-up a dream to you as a child, and shopping a "day at Disneyland" type of experience? If so, I shall like to welcome you to the Light Plane Fashion School. At least give you a tiny glimpse into what goes on here on the "other side" when it comes to fashion.

For you may wonder if we even dress here. It may seem quite dull if we don't! I am here to tell you that we do have our own manner of dress here, and that we do study fashion to the nth degree, shall we say! For fashion is as ethereal and lovely and inspiring as the next pursuit!

Now that I've gotten that out of the way, as they say, what more shall I tell you about fashion, fashion, fashion?

Well, for one, developing your own style is quite a grand thing in the fashion world. I most certainly did that as Audrey. When you develop your own style, you do express yourself to the nth degree. You do! And it is quite glorious for us to see from here. I assure you.

If you've developed your own style, you may have questions about whether you've gotten it "right," or if there is more for you to do. Well, I do have to say there is always more to do. For there is always more utterly divine dresses and frocks and shoes to wear. And for men, more simply divine "outfits," as well. But I am digressing. I am only meaning to say that the fashion realm will forever be changing. It truly is a living and breathing type of "animal," shall we say—though a most divinely gorgeous one—like a sleek panther.

But let's return to your own style. What if you haven't yet developed much of a style? Or what if you haven't identified your style? What then?

Well, for one, I would urge you to know that you do indeed have a style. You just need to access it. That is all, and yet that isn't as easy as it may sound.

How might you access your style? Here are some pointers—numbered—just for you!

1. What do you truly like? What would you wear with abandon and flair if you weren't concerned about the opinions of others? For that gives you a BIG clue to your personal style. Do use that item of clothing, or hat, or gloves, or shoes, or entire outfit as your barometer of what makes your style you!

2. Figure out how you can incorporate what you see in your mind's eye into your wardrobe. Be that a certain dress with a particular cut and material and color. Or a type of shoe. Or a certain type of accessory.

3. Get courageous with your clothing! "Go out on a limb" with your clothing—and then jump off the limb. This will get you exactly where you wish to go with your fashion character and sense.

4. Know that whatever you choose to wear, you can most certainly change tomorrow. You can! You need only make a few or a lot of changes to your attire. That is all!

5. Jumping off the thought in number 4. Keep in mind that there are no mistakes in the fashion realm. There are only experiments!!! If you keep that in mind, you will find yourself trying out bolder and bolder fashion trends and styles—you just will! And that will be quite grand.

6. Ask for help from us in the Light Plane Fashion School. Others have said this, and I do repeat. We will be right next to you in a quick, hot moment. Before you know it, you will be applying a certain shade of lipstick and choosing a certain piece of jewelry or shoes. And it will look quite smashing, as they say!

And for you men, you will suddenly simply have to slide on a certain pant and combine it with a certain shirt and tie for a big event. You will feel compelled and elated when you let us help you! And we will feel quite pleased to assist!

That's it for me! I'm off to teach a class in the Light Plane Fashion School.
Tata to you, and kisses always!
Audrey Hepburn

———∞———

AUDREY HEPBURN was a Belgian-British actress born on May 4, 1929. She died at the age of 63, due to appendiceal cancer, on January 20, 1993. In addition to her acting ability, Hepburn was known for her distinctive fashion sense and style. She made the International Best Dressed Hall of Fame list in 1961. This honor is given to individuals with a style sensibility considered to stand the test of time. The list was founded by fashionista Eleanor Lambert (#18). Hepburn was born in Belgium to Dutch baroness Ella Van Heemstra and Joseph Victor Anthony Ruston. Her father left the family when she was six. During World War II, Hepburn lived in the Netherlands. Her mother felt it would be safer, because it was a neutral country. Still, Hepburn endured hardship during that time in Nazi-occupied Holland, including malnutrition. She did, however, attend school and took ballet lessons. After the war, she continued ballet lessons, as well as studied acting and worked as a model and dancer in London. She was a graceful, striking model and felt that she'd found her calling, until she was spotted while modeling by a film producer. Before long, she was an international superstar. Hepburn was also a philanthropist. She served as a goodwill ambassador for UNICEF.

18

✦ ELEANOR LAMBERT ✦

Hello! So proud to present here, and to be included. Eleanor Lambert here, at your "fashion service."

I would like to talk to you today/tonight about making a living in the fashion world. For many of you reading are thinking about entering the fashion realm in one way or another and may very well be asking if it's possible to "make any money at it," as they say.

Well, I was one who did figure out how to make money with fashion—as a fashion publicist. So, I can honestly say to you that there is quite a lot of money to be made in fashion. For various reasons. For one, people will always try to look their absolute best. And others may try to look even better than their absolute best. I make this last comment somewhat in jest, and yet I also say this with wisdom coming from many years as a fashion maven. A maven who dished out fashion advice—particularly about becoming the next greatest fashion sensation!

So, what should you do if you wish to make a ton of money from fashion? Well, the first step may surprise you. Nothing. For there is a lot more manifesting in the process than there is in the doing. Fashion is a sort of ethereal thing, shall we say. By that I mean that what is considered beautiful and fashionable does seem to come from the ether at times.

Truly, those in the industry will put something out there and wait to see if it will stick, shall we say. Be it short-shorts or suspenders or midriff attire, or even the dreaded "highwater look," there is truly at times no rhyme or reason to what occurs. Hence, planning can be a bit off-putting and confusing, even.

Okay, so I hope that I haven't dissuaded you from pursuing a lovely career in fashion. For fashion is quite grand! Most certainly, I did love fashion as Eleanor. I could and did quite literally eat, sleep, and breathe fashion, fashion, fashion.

I mentioned doing nothing to get things going. Well, of course, you won't exactly be doing nothing. Your fingers and feet and toes and elbows may not be doing much, but your mind and heart will most certainly be whirring. And this is what I would like you to do when that occurs. I would like you to work on letting your heart and head marry—letting them meld on the topic of fashion.

What occurs when you allow this to happen? Why, you may have already guessed that what occurs is that your heart does sing to your mind and gives your mind the verve and wherewithal to get a move on. And then your mind does do its own whirring and comes up with some absolutely spectacular ideas about how to make quite a splash in the fashion realm. That way you become noticed and compensated for your divine fashion ideas.

I know, this is a little "out there," this advice. But then I am here in the Light. That being said, I shall like to give you a few pointers for how to ensure that you do make a success of your time in the fashion world. Here we shall go.

1. Be prudent. By this I mean, don't try on out in public in front of potential fans every possible fashion item or opportunity that comes your way. Do take a step back, if you are a model, for instance, and are asked to model a rather unsightly outfit. I do understand that if you have signed on to take a job that you must then put on said outfit. But if you know what will be modeled in a particular show and don't think it is well-suited for you, do bow out gracefully. For the camera—in particular—can't un-see certain things. I do think you know of what I speak!

2. Keep an open mind. I know this seems a bit odd to mention this to you in regards to fashion, but I think you do understand this on a certain level. There are many odd things out there—but then sometimes those odd things (think knickerbockers) do have their place. And they may even have quite a big place. Do try to remain objective, while also adhering to point #1 (prudence).

3. Study the masters. Those in your area of the fashion realm. For they certainly got to where they got by knowing a few—or a lot—of things! So, do study their lives and their careers and their choices, even. You will find that treasures await when you do so.

4. Be patient. I know this is something that you probably don't want to hear, but a fashion career can indeed take some time to build. Behind all of those "overnight sensations" you will find many, many, many long days and nights working and striving, and sometimes failing!

5. Know. Know that you are exactly where you are meant to be in the fashion realm. That everything you wish for will come to you, should you wait until the perfect time for everything to occur. Just as you can't rush a good perm or hair straightening or alteration for a dress, you can't rush your fashion career.

6. Have faith. I know this seems a lot like #5, but this is quite different. Have faith that you have made the right choice in choosing fashion. At the same time, have faith that you will continue to make all the right choices. That you will know when to curtsy, that you will know when to bow, that you will know what color combo is best in an

75

ensemble, and that you will know what to say about a dress for which you are receiving compliments. In short, trust yourself to make all the right divinely inspired fashion decisions. And if you ever doubt, do call on us fashion experts in the Light for assistance!

Good day to you always. May you find what you're looking for in your divine fashion closet of life!
    Always,
    Eleanor Lambert

ELEANOR LAMBERT BERKSON was an American fashion publicist born on August 10, 1903. She died at the age of 100 on October 7, 2003. Lambert was known for her tireless promotion of American fashion over several decades. This promotion elevated the American fashion industry from rags to riches. Dubbed the "Empress of Seventh Avenue," Lambert was known for wearing turbans and oversized jewelry. She worked tirelessly to publicize the work of a wide variety of American designers, including Bill Blass (#22), Oscar de la Renta (#7), and Anne Klein (#32). Lambert founded the Council of Fashion Designers of America in 1962, which she ran for more than a decade. She had a keen eye for spotting rising fashion designers, including Halston. Known for speaking her mind and not taking no for an answer, Lambert disagreed with the editors of *Harper's Bazaar* and *Vogue* in the 1940s and 1950s for their focus on Paris as the fashion design capital. Her efforts at publicizing the work of American designers got them more and more attention over time. According to her longtime friend John Loring, her motto was: "Don't look back." Lambert also founded New York Fashion Week, the Met Gala, and the International Best Dressed List.

19

❧ PAUL MITCHELL ❧

Hello there! Paul Mitchell here. So ultra-glad to present!! Here we shall go!

Hair, hair, hair, hair, hair, hair, hair, hair, hair!! Did I say hair! What a glorious substance is hair! I so loved hair in my lifetime as Paul. I did!

The feel of hair. The way it tumbles down a woman's—or a man's—back! The silky-smooth way that hair can feel when hair is well cared for! Hair, hair, hair, hair, hair!! Oh, my!

Will I go on and on about hair here? Yes, and no. For I do wish to give you some nuggets of my wisdom, such as it is here in the Light—about your hair care!

How shall you go about caring for your hair, so that your hair does have a most glossy sheen? While there are certainly mousses and mixes and the like that can do that for you, there are a few things you can most certainly do yourself. I shall talk of them here.

I do suggest putting pure, real avocado paste in your hair. Do get yourself a ripe avocado or two—mash it up in a food processor, and then do apply it to your hair, until your hair is completely covered. Put your hair in a plastic shower cap or a plastic bag, and let it sit for 30 minutes. Then rinse your hair out well with lukewarm water. You will also need to wash it. Use a mild, phosphate-free shampoo.

Apply avocado to your hair monthly, and you shall begin to see a most lustrous shine coming from your hair. The avocado works from the inside out nourishing your glorious strands of hair. You shall be so glad that you did this after about the sixth time!

Drink tons and tons of water. Water, water, water is good for your hair, hair, hair. It does get into the follicles, all that water, it just does. There is a science behind all of this, but this isn't a scientific book. Suffice it to say that the water does do your hair good—and your scalp, which is where the follicles lie! I think you see what I am saying.

Watch the types of products you use. Opt for phosphate-free whenever possible. And natural fragrances, not harsh ones. For the harsher the products you use, the harder on your hair they shall be!

Do watch the consumption of junk food. While junk food is most certainly okay in doses, a diet of such is not recommended! The trouble is not so much the junk food, but the fact that it is devoid of nutrients, which your hair does require. Fill yourself up on junk food, and you shall not fill up your hair and its follicles with good-for-you stuff!

Wash regularly, but not too often. While it certainly is a good thing to wash your hair when it is dirty, it is not a good thing to wash your hair when it is only slightly dirty, or just because it's Tuesday. Do try to back off on washing, if possible, if you are washing every day.

Now on to styling! I did so love the styling as Paul! Hot implements are, of course, to be limited. As they do burn the hair, and that can cause damage and will most definitely take away some of the shine, too! I do know that at times hot is what is required to get a certain look, so I won't tell you to never use hot curlers and irons—just do use them judiciously!

When you do style your hair, while I would suggest going by current fashion standards, if that's what you like, don't do so if you aren't enamored with any of the styles. For the truth is, if you love your style, you will love your hair! That's just generally the way it goes! So, wear a style from a year ago, or a decade ago, if that's what you like!

One last thing before I go! Do know that we watch over your hair from here—us fashionistas for hair. So, if you would like some styling or grooming or care tips, please do ask. We are very happy to oblige!

Good day to you! And have fun, fun, fun with your fabulous hair, hair, hair!

Yours,

Paul Mitchell

———⬤⬤⬤———

CYRIL THOMSON MITCHELL (Paul Mitchell) was a Scottish-American hairstylist and entrepreneur born on January 27, 1936. He died at the age of 53, due to pancreatic cancer, on April 21, 1989. Mitchell is most known for being the co-founder of the haircare product company, John Paul Mitchell Systems. He started the company in 1980 with John Paul DeJoria. In 2000, he founded Paul Mitchell the School, which now has more than 100 locations. He is known for creating and making popular wash-and-wear hairstyles, which were supported with his various products. Mitchell was born in Scotland and spent his formative years in England. He originally trained to be a silversmith but decided to follow in his mother's footsteps. She was a hairdresser. When Mitchell was 16, he began studying at the Morris School of Hairdressing in London. By 18, he'd won numerous British and international hairdressing competitions. In 1954, he began going by the name Paul, given to him by his first boss, at a salon where he earned 12 pounds a week. In 1960, he went to work for Vidal Sassoon's (#15) salon in London. Mitchell was invited to the US in 1965 and decided to stay to train staff in Sassoon's first salon in America. Mitchell met DeJoria in 1971, and they became fast friends. The next year, he opened Superhair Salon. By 1973, hairdressers from across the US were coming for training from Mitchell during his Paul Mitchell Cutting Club events. In 1974, he had an opportunity to do trainings in Hawaii. He sold the

Superhair Salon in 1976 and moved to Hawaii to host week-long seminars. In 1980, he and DeJoria launched their revolutionary haircare system with just $700. Mitchell and De Joria started a self-sustaining, solar-powered awapuhi farm in Hawaii in 1983. It is a species of plant in the ginger family and is still used in the Paul Mitchell products today. When he passed, Mitchell left his share of the company to his son, Angus.

20

❧ GLORIA VANDERBILT ❧

Hello! Utterly happy to connect. Gloria Vanderbilt here! I am not long here in the Light from my lifetime as Gloria, however, I am thrilled to be included! So here we shall go!

Utter, stupendous fashion!! Oh, my, what a glorious, glorious world is the fashion world! Truly so many glorious things to admire in the fashion world. Like dresses and suits and shoes and handbags and belts, even. And then there is even the mannequins used on which to put the fashionable merchandise! I was and still am quite literally thrilled with fashion!

Okay, so I have showed you how much I adore fashion. Now what shall you tell them, Gloria! Well, for one, I would like to urge you to follow your heart when it comes to fashion. For if fashion fuels your soul, then do let fashion fuel your soul! Please don't (this is all free will, of course!)—but please don't push away the fashion bug for something more "respectable" like accounting or business development or even organization. While these are certainly all wonderful fields, and they are being covered in additional volumes in this series, if these occupations or any others aren't for you, they simply are not for you!! However, if fashion does make your heart and soul sing, then FASHION IS MOST CERTAINLY FOR YOU!! I SHALL ADD TO THIS A WOO HOO, as I've seen others do here.

Okay, so you have agreed—at least at the moment—to follow your fashion inspiration and your love for fashion. What next?

Do refrain from worrying or fretting about how you will "make it" in the fashion world and how you will put "food" on the proverbial table. Am I suggesting that you don't find ways and means by which to feed yourself and feed the thrill that you get from fashion—such as a part-time bookkeeping job, as Dear Julie did do as she built up her writing career many years ago? You can most certainly tell by this sentence that I do urge you to pay for what you need in whatever manner works for you. However, at the same time, do burn some midnight oil, as they say, sewing up delightful fashions or drawing them or conceiving them, or whatever it is that makes your heart and soul sing!!! For that is the secret, as they say, to getting you to where you wish to go with fashion, fashion, fashion!!

What else shall I tell you now that I can give you "lofty" ideas from "up here" in the Light? Perhaps I shall add to the paragraph above with some meatier tips that you can most likely sink your needle into!!

Do work hard at this fashion thing. Yes, it is necessary. While you may be gifted, and you may be inspired, and you may have tons of delight at the prospect of going into the fashion industry, at the same time, it is critical that you also harness the incredible amounts of energy that do come from those prior three mentioned attributes—for you will most certainly need it!! There is much to do in the fashion realm, as there is in many realms, and there is much "grunt" work, even. So, do know that if you wish to "make it," you will need to put in a lot of elbow grease, as they say. Though do use caution with that grease amongst the various glorious textiles that you are working with!!

Don't give up. Don't take no for an answer. If doors are closed on you and your fashion ideas or yourself as a model, do go to the next door and the next and the next, until a door does open, and you're invited to step through. For I can guarantee you that inside one of those doors you will most certainly find a glorious rainbow, and that rainbow is a bridge that will take you to the next rainbow and the next pile of riches in the fashion realm! There will most certainly be dark times when you wonder "what on Earth" (pun intended) you are doing!! And if you should just give up and become a full-time accountant, for crying out loud! But if you knock on just one more door, you may discover the sweet spot in your fashion journey and reach new, great heights. So, do keep going!!!

I do have quite a bit to say on this topic, as you can see. Specifically, on the topic of following your heart and your dreams in the fashion realm and embracing all the loveliness of the fashion realm!! I am going to say goodbye for now. But do know that I am at your beck and call regarding fashion at any time. Now that I am in the Light, I am quite literally available to anyone who loves fashion 24/7!!!

Good day to you always, and best wishes on your fashion journey!
Yours,
Gloria Vanderbilt

GLORIA LAURA VANDERBILT was an American fashion designer, artist, author, and heiress/socialite born on February 20, 1924. She died at the age of 95, due to stomach cancer, on June 17, 2019. Vanderbilt made a name for herself in the fashion industry when she launched a line of fashion, perfumes, and household goods bearing her name. This started the concept of celebrity branding. She was also the first designer to make a fashion statement using jeans. In her hands, the once lowly, casual garment became tight-fitting designer items soon worn by celebrities and the public. Vanderbilt was a member of the Vanderbilt family of New York. Her father died when she was young, and her mother ended up in a highly-publicized court battle with her aunt over custody of her. Her aunt was awarded custody, and Vanderbilt ended up having a difficult childhood. Vanderbilt's career in fashion began when she was 15 years old when she appeared in *Harper's Bazaar*. It was during the 1970s that she launched her fashion business, which started with her licensing her name and some of her paintings on a line of scarves. In 1976, the tight-fitting jeans that became her trademark were released featuring her signature and swan logo embroidered on the back pocket. The jeans were an immediate sensation. Vanderbilt was married four times. She is the mother of CNN journalist and television anchor Anderson Cooper. She also wrote a variety of books, including memoirs.

21

⤳ ALEXANDRE DE PARIS ⬳

Hello there! Alexandre de Paris here. Come to talk about hair. Glorious, utterly divine hair!

I so loved a good hairstyle as Alexandre. So, that is what I will discuss here. How to come up with the "best" hairstyle for you!

First, I do suggest having an open mind. For the right hairstyle for you may not be the right hairstyle in the mind of your hairdresser. Does that mean that if your hairdresser doesn't understand your "vision" when it comes to your hairstyle that you should not use him or her? Generally, it isn't necessary to "fire" your hairdresser, but you do want the person to listen to what you want and then ultimately give you what you want. I'm sure you will agree!!

So, what shall you do to determine the right style for you?

It does help to look at some styles. Do this by looking through a book of styles at the hairdressers, or do look at styles online, as you can today. As you look at the styles, do pay particular attention to those styles that you immediately like and that do stop you, so that you stare.

While some styles may not be feasible for your particular hair, do think about what it is you like about those styles. It may be the way the style frames your face, or it may be the particular cut, or it may be the overall look. I say to pay careful attention to this, for those types of hints could help you and your stylist come up with a similar style that does your hair justice.

Whatever you do when you seek out a style for your utterly divine head of hair, refrain from self-editing as you look. For instance, refrain from telling yourself you are too old for a style, or too short, etc. Because the truth is, as you've heard here already, when you utterly love a style, the style will love you, and you will be ecstatic about your hair. Truly, the best absolute thing is that you feel utterly excited about your hairstyle! It doesn't matter how others feel. The hair is on your head, and the style is what you wear around all day and night! Okay?!!

Next, do try out a variety of hair-dos. For that is how you will come up with just the right style for you, you, you! The more you experiment (within reason), the more you will know exactly what it is you wish to do with your lovely tresses!

What else? How about this. How about if you suspend disbelief. By this I mean that you refrain from believing that your hair has limitations. For if you do this, you will be surprised at what can be done with your hair. This does harken back to what I said prior about finding out what hair looks you like and then finding styles that will mimic those looks.

What else?

I suggest that you do embrace everything hair. Do look at as much as you can about hair. Do delve into the depths of haircare and how you can have the healthiest hair possible. Some of my contemporaries here, such as dear Paul Mitchell (#19), do give you some great tips for hair care. Listen to those tips!! Do!!! For they will help you maintain the best possible hair that you can! Hair that can be styled into your dream look!

When you wish to go elegant—please do so! And ask for my divine assistance. For that was certainly one of my specialties as Alexandre. Elegant, fabulous hairstyles!! I did excel at them, and I do wish to share their divinity with you now! Ask for me to come in to help you personally with your styling, and you shall be amazed!

That is all from me for today. I do have a few things to attend to in the Light Plane Hair Fashion School that I help direct. Good day— or night—to you always!

    Yours truly, truly, and ever so devoutly,

    Alexandre de Paris

—⟨∞⟩—

LOUIS ALEXANDRE RAIMON (Alexandre de Paris) was a French hairdresser born on September 6, 1922. He died at the age of 85 on January 3, 2008. Raimon was well known for styling the hair of famous actresses, including creating Elizabeth Taylor's hairstyle for the 1963 Hollywood epic film *Cleopatra*. He also styled Greta Garbo, Lauren Bacall, and Audrey Hepburn. One of his signatures was the chignon at the back of the head. Raimon began working as an apprentice in a hair salon in the French Riviera in 1938. Soon thereafter, he became the apprentice of his mentor, Antoine de Paris. There he met Andrée Banaudi, whom he married. In 1946, he created the chignon. It soon became an art form and featured various twists. At a 1961 dinner given in France for President John F. Kennedy, he put diamonds in Jackie Kennedy's chignon. For more than 40 years, Raimon worked with French haute couture masters, including Christian Dior (#33), Karl Lagerfeld (#12), Coco Chanel (#6), and Yves Saint-Laurent (#3). He also opened his own salon with partners in 1952, and then went solo in 1957. Raimon's clientele included royalty, such as the Duchess of Windsor, Princess Grace of Monaco, and Queen Sirikit of Thailand.

22

⇒ Bill Blass ⇐

Hello! Bill Blass here. Come to talk to you about glorious fashion, and how you might fit into the fashion puzzle of life! Let us begin.

Where shall I begin when I speak to you of fashion? Well, for one, I do wish you a glorious time enjoying fashion on the Earth Plane. For I must tell you that the divine clothing on the Earth Plane is utterly divine. It simply is! There are few places in the Universe where you can enjoy a good look at a glorious frock or gown or suit or lovely hairdo! Certainly, the Earth Plane is the place to see and enjoy glorious, glorious fashion!

Okay, so I have waxed on about fashion. I have gone on and on, as you might say, about how lovely fashion and all its components can be. Now what on Earth can I tell you!

How about this? How about that you enjoy fashion for fashion's sake, and that you try on a variety of fashions as you go. I am referring to fashions that you wear on the body and fashions that you give to your lovely tresses.

Do try various fashions. Even fashions that don't seem to be "you." For when you do this, it is much like taking a few different types of courses in college. You discover out of pure luck or coincidence that certain fashions just may be for you. Or at least certain fashions may have a bit of this or that, which you'd like to wear a little more of.

And what of hair? Since it was my forte as Bill Blass? Well, I shall tell you this right now. Do let your hair do what it will do—within reason, of course. What I mean by this is that if you choose to try various fashions with your hair—do so! However, for the most comfortable and easy to care for styles, do go with what your hair wishes to do. For instance, if you have a stubborn "cowlick" that wants to go a certain way—do go its way! Do that with your do (ha ha!) For that will make your life a lot easier, I assure you. Especially when you are attempting to get your hair done in a jiffy so that you can get out of the house to an appointment!

That being said, it is often a lovely idea to have hairdos that work for a quick put together and those that you toil over for a most magnificent look. This isn't to say that the do you create for your "everyday" do isn't a lovely one—it's just not one that you put your whole fashion heart and soul into!

When you curl your hair, if you so choose, do let the curl curl where it may, as well. For there are ways that your hair wishes to create a ringlet or a wavy curl—there just are! You most likely know which way that would be, yet when styling you try to "wrestle" your tresses, so to speak, to do what you wish. And then what do you know! They boing back onto place—into their place—not the one you would like. So, do "give in" to your hair's wishes—at least some of the time—and you will make your hairstyling easier and more productive and successful!

Washing your hair. I know this has been said before by others, and I shall say it again now. Do try to use high-quality shampoo—preferably from your hairdresser. I know there are perfectly good brands out and about at the store, as you say, but you can be assured of a good quality product at your local hairdresser. This is of much importance if you have treated hair or hair that is thinning or thin. And now that I'm not on the Earth Plane, I can honestly say that I say this out of a true concern for the health and longevity of your hair—not because I shall be getting a "kickback" from a shampoo and conditioner manufacturer!

What else?

I will leave you with this. The fashion realm does love you. It truly does. I know there is a bit of a feeling of not ever being truly, utterly fashionable—like another—when you do focus on your own beauty. That is a human trait, and a human challenge, most certainly! At the same time, it truly isn't necessary to compare yourself to anyone—not even yourself!! For your everlasting beauty—which it is—will be with you indefinitely. Do be kind to yourself, and do celebrate your absolutely, positively glorious beauty—inner and outer, of course!

That is all from me for now. I do wish you a glorious time enjoying the fashion realm on Earth at this time.
Good Day!
Bill Blass

———— ⊗⊗⊗ ————

WILLIAM RALPH BLASS (Bill Blass) was an American fashion designer born on June 22, 1922. He died at the age of 79, due to cancer, on June 12, 2002. Blass is known for his contribution to the laidback, simple elegance of American fashion created in the late 20th Century. His fashion designs became popular with high-society women in New York following World War II. Born in Indiana, Blass knew he wanted to design clothing from an early age. He left home after high school, moving to New York where he found a job as a sketch artist for a sportwear firm. He took a break to serve in the US Army during World War II. Afterwards, he joined the New York fashion house of Anna Miller and Co. In 1959, when the company merged with Maurice Rentner, Ltd., he became the head designer for Rentner. Prior to Blass's designs, Rentner had produced high-priced matronly looking clothing for "amply proportioned" women. Blass produced the clothing with a young look, and the buying public loved the designs. This catapulted Blass up the ladder at the company, where he eventually reached partner. His designs were known for simple lines, quality fabric and superior tailoring, mixed with brilliant colors and the ability to mix and match various patterns. By 1963, Blass was a celebrated designer with customers such as Marilyn Monroe (#2) and Jacqueline Kennedy. Blass became owner of Rentner in 1970 and renamed the company after himself, licensing his creations and creating a franchising subsidiary. In addition to women's clothing, Blass designed children's and menswear, rainwear, swimsuits, furs, shoes, gloves, scarves, jewelry, hosier, and luggage. His company is still thriving today.

———⊗⊗⊗———

"Something about glamour interested me. All my schoolbooks had drawings of women on terraces with a cocktail and a cigarette."
—Bill Blass

23

❧ Mario Prada ❦

Hello there! Mario Prada here. The original founder of Prada.
Pleased to present! Here we shall go.

How exciting is the fashion life! I know others have said this, and I say it again. Of course, as Mario I was rather intrigued with leather goods. For one, it was quite long ago at the turn of the prior century. So, leather was a common material for items such as purses. For two, I so loved the scent of fresh leather—especially when the leather was fashioned into something quite divine, such as a leather bag, or purse, or shoes.

What is it about leather? Truly? What is it? Of course, nowadays you do have the alternatives to leather. Some manmade. And they truly can be quite lovely—especially when dyed to perfection, as they often can be! But leather—true leather—is unlike any other substance. It ranks right up there with silk in my book, in terms of being a rather enduring and lovely material with which to work.

Does that mean you should always get leather products, and/or design with leather, rather than other materials, such as manmade? No, it doesn't. Although, I would urge you to look for and use those substances with the least amount of processing. At least for the most part. For those are the materials that will truly shine in your collection. For instance, if you create your own clothing and introduce your own line. The natural feel and the natural look of natural clothing truly can't be beat!

What else shall I tell you? Well, I would like to share what I do think of when I create for the public. For I am still creating, in a sense, and then sharing the information. And I did create quite a bit before my "demise" on the Earth Plane. Though I have to say that my work was carried on by my daughter and now my granddaughter in a quite grand manner!

When creating for the general public—think generally. This may sound like matter-of-fact, simple and straightforward advice—and indeed it is. For it is when you think simply that you shall come up with some genius designs.

Ask yourself the following question when striving to come up with the next best wonderful design.

1. What do people want with_____? Fill in the item of clothing or fashion accessory. Jump on the first thing that comes to mind, for that is the answer to your question as to what to create next. Of course, if you come up with something that has already been done, do think of variations of that. Do think about the essence of your thought. Look closely at the fact that is presented. For instance— people want comfort. What type of clothing or fashion accessory that you've been creating springs to mind? How could you make your item more comfortable? Or how could you make your item representative of the ultimate in comfort?

2. Get crazy. I don't mean go crazy. I mean get crazy. Go a little zany with your designing. Feeling a little stumped? Jump up and down and shake up the thoughts in your head, and then go back to the proverbial drawing board. Take a quick run around the block or the office. Then jump back into your work and record whatever crazy idea is in your head. You just might find yourself a winner this way!

3. Connect. While creating and designing as much as possible is a good thing, you also want to get out there and network, as you say in your day. Network with others in the industry, while you also network with potential customers. The more you connect, the more connected you will be with what people want to wear and use for accessories.

4. Study. Study the masters of design—from fashion designers to those individuals with their own personal sense of style. Take apart and analyze what makes their products and/or designs work. Look at the models of yesteryear and today. How do they wear the clothing? How do they make the clothing jump out at you and grab you by the coattails and not let you go?

5. Fear not. Avoid worrying yourself about if you're on the right track, and if your work is going to do well. Just design. Push away any thoughts of anxiety or distraction and just create, create, create! Doing so will get you exactly where you wish to go! And all your fashion design dreams are sure to come true!

> *That's all from me for now. I do feel honored to have been asked to present here. I am grateful for your patronage and admiration all these years of the great work started by me and carried on by my heirs!*
>
> *Yours Truly,*
> *Mario Prada*

MARIO PRADA was an Italian fashion designer. He died in 1958. Prada founded the fashion design label Prada. He was the original designer of the company that specializes in high fashion goods for men and women. This includes handbags, luggage, shoes, and other leather goods. Prada started the company in 1913 with his brother, Martino. The duo started the company as a leather goods shop. At the time, the shop sold leather goods, including handbags, and English steamer trunks. Aristocrats began visiting his shop and buying his merchandise. In 1919, Prada was recognized as an official supplier to the Italian Royal House. That is how the coat of arms and knotted rope of the House of Savoy became a part of the Prada logo.

24

➤ KATE SPADE ◄

Hi, there! Kate Spade here. Come to talk fashion. Let's get this thing up, up, and away! Hooray!

One of the things I like about being "up here" in the Light. I can say whatever I wish—within reason, of course!

That being said, do you say whatever you wish with your fashion statements? With your attire and your makeup and hair? Do you dare say what you wish to say? I'm here to tell you this now—and I know it's "easy" for me to say, since I'm here and you're there—but I'm here to tell you to go ahead and stand up for what you believe in terms of your attire! Go ahead and be you. Just do it, already! For when you do, you will look quite divine and totally incredible in whatever you choose to wear!

Does this advice go a little or a lot against what I would have said as Kate? Perhaps. But then again, who cares! For I'm here now, as I mentioned, and you so well know. And now I'm telling you to be yourself. Be your true fashion self. For when you do, your inner and outer beauty will surely shine through.

That means that if you wish to wear a hat, then do wear a hat. If you wish to wear a certain color and it isn't "in" at the moment—know that it's certainly okay to do so. And certainly, the color will come back in again sooner or later!

I'd also like to take this opportunity to discuss purses. I know my

96

dear friend Étienne Aigner (#10) did a great job at that, but I have my own "things" to tell you about purses.

First, purses are, of course, absolutely divine. What an incredible invention, wouldn't you agree? You can put so much in a purse, and you can also use it as a stylish accessory. Certainly, purses do deserve a lot of attention when you are planning an outfit and even when you are planning an entire wardrobe!

So, do pay careful and special attention to your purses. Look at the style of each purse and the material and the cut and how the purse does hang from your hand or shoulder. Certainly, think of purses as you would any other item of clothing. And don't forget color!!! The color of your purses so deserves attention. For think of how you can pair your purse color with your shoe color. That is absolutely magnificent when it is done well!!

Okay, enough about purses, I hear you saying. What more shall you tell us Kate? Pearls of wisdom about beauty, please, please, please, Kate! About accessing beauty. Fine, I shall tell you. I shall give you a little bit of wisdom in this regard!

The beauty is in the eye of the beholder. That is most certainly true. But the beauty is more than skin deep. The beauty is on the surface and the beauty is under the surface, and the beauty is in how you talk about the beauty. For when you say good things to yourself and to others about their appearance, you will notice that things become more beautiful. Think of this. How often have you seen it happen that a gaggle of women do gather around a baby and they do talk about how cute the baby is. While all babies are cute in their own right—that is for sure—the baby being talked about does begin to glow. The baby does begin to look cuter and cuter and cuter—until everyone gazing upon the little girl or boy is swooning!

Am I saying that your attitude about what you look like does affect what you look like? Yes, I am! So, when you look in the mirror, do swoon over what you see!!! Praise your reflection and your reflection will praise you and glow with an inner and an outer beauty like you've never seen before.

> *That's all for me. I do hope I have helped and that I haven't confused you too much!*
> *Yours Truly,*
> *Kate Spade*

KATHERINE NOEL VALENTINE BROSNAHAN (Kate Spade) was an American fashion designer and businesswoman born on December 24, 1962. She died at the age of 55, due to suicide, on June 5, 2018. Spade founded and owned the brand, Kate Spade New York. She started with stylish and sophisticated, yet functional handbags, eventually adding to her line clothing, shoes, jewelry and accessories, as well as home goods like towels and china. Spade grew up in Kansas City, Missouri where she attended an all-girl Catholic school. She went to college in Kansas and then transferred to Arizona State University where she earned a degree in journalism. She originally intended to become a television producer. Spade also always enjoyed fashion. It was while working in the accessories department at *Mademoiselle* magazine in Manhattan that Spade (then going by Katy Brosnahan) began living with Andy Spade, whom she had met in Arizona when the two worked in a men's clothing store. Spade left the magazine in 1991 as a senior fashion editor with the idea of creating her own handbags. While at *Mademoiselle*, she'd noted the lack of stylish and sensible handbags on the market. She made handbag prototypes with tape and paper, and a manufacturer in New York made them into actual bags. The couple launched the company and named it combining her first name with his last name. Her idea to put the label on the outside of the bag established the brand. Priced from $150-$450, the bags flew off the shelves. In 1996, the brand opened its first boutique in Manhattan's SoHo district, eventually moving to a bigger facility. She launched her Kate Spade at Home collection in 2004, also publishing books on fashion, etiquette, and entertaining later that year. Spade sold a portion of her business to the Neiman Marcus Group in 1999 and the remainder in 2006. She decided to focus on raising the daughter she had with Andy in 2005. In 2016, she started the company Frances Valentine, specializing in luxury handbags and footwear.

25

❧ REEVA STEENKAMP ❧

Hello! Reeva here. Come to talk to you about the fabulous world of beauty, beauty, beauty! Let us begin.

I so loved being a model. What an absolutely charming and uplifting profession. Certainly, there were times when it was difficult and did show the "underbelly" of society—but for the most part, it was a magical adventure being a model. For where else can you become someone else, in a sense, through a wardrobe, and at the same time share with the world the essence of beauty itself? Certainly, being a model is a noble profession! It is. And few can "carry it off" in a manner that pleases many!

This is not to say that all models aren't truly divine creatures. Female and male models included! This is only to say that it does take a "special" person to be a very successful model. I don't say this to disparage anyone at all. I only say this for those of you reading this who wish to become models or know someone who wishes to. For I would like to give you a few pointers about the modeling life and becoming a model and staying happy being a model. Here we go with my advice, such as it is!

1. Be ready. Be ready to face your inner beauty and your outer beauty. Be ready to bare your soul. For when you pose for an audience on a runway, and for the camera, you do show a little or a lot of yourself. Many models don't realize how this can make you feel quite vulnerable—for good reason—until they experience it. Do be ready to be vulnerable.

2. Have faith. In you and your abilities and in mankind. Have faith that whoever is supposed to see you and what you are wearing and selling will do so. Have faith that your superiors, in terms of bosses and makeup artists, will know that you are indeed doing your absolute best, and that your absolute best is more than good enough!

3. Preen. Yes, I said it! Go ahead and preen in front of the mirror. You know you want to, so go ahead and do it! Certainly, preening is good practice for when you appear in front of the camera and on the runway and red carpet. Preening gives you confidence, and preening teaches you good timing, which is something that is vital in the world of modeling. It's often said that timing is necessary for musicians and for comedians. Well, I am here to tell you that timing is essential for models as well!

4. Practice. I know this does harken back to the former tip a bit, but it bears repeating. Practice makes close to perfect. It just does! Practice smiling for the camera and posing, and practice letting go and exposing your inner beauty for the world to see. Practice until you are tired of practicing, and then practice some more!

5. Believe. Believe that you can and will become successful. That is the only way to the top, so to speak, in the modeling realm. Disbelief in your abilities will lead to disbelief across the board. And that won't help you reach your goals. So, believe, believe, believe, and be happy that you do believe!

6. Take good care of yourself. Yes, I know. There are models who eat a bite of apple a day and stay out all night partying. But you will find that those sorts of lifestyles will catch up to you. Often sooner than later! So, do eat right. Fresh produce galore and lean proteins. And do drink tons of calorie-free real water. And get your beauty sleep!

7. Embrace your fans. Within reason, of course. But do reach out and thank your fans for following you. The more you reach out in gratitude, the more fans you will gather along the way.

8. Ignore the criticism. Of course, you will have criticism along the way. About your weight, most definitely, and about little, seemingly minor things about your person. For the world will pick apart, so to speak, you as they do adore you at the same time. That being said, there will be very little rhyme or reason to criticism. So, ignore most of it. And when you do get some valid criticism, simply thank the Universe for it, and do what you think is best to rectify whatever situation is being presented to you. Okay!!

Thank you for listening. I have gone on a bit here, and I am grateful that the opportunity came up. For not everyone who "auditioned" for this book made it in. But that is as it should be, and another thing for you to remember. You won't "win" every audition. You know this. But do know that you will win the right auditions. Okay! Now get to your fabulous day!!!
Yours Sincerely,
Reeva Steenkamp

REEVA STEENKAMP was a South African model born on August 19, 1983. She died at the age of 29, due to gunshot wounds, on February 14, 2013. Steenkamp is best known as the first face of Avon cosmetics in South Africa. She also modeled for *FHM* magazine and starred in various television advertisements for brands such as Toyota. Born in

Cape Towne, Steenkamp's father was a horse trainer. She was an avid rider until she broke her back during a fall while riding in her early 20s and had to learn to walk again. After graduating from high school, Steenkamp studied law with the plan of becoming a lawyer by age 30. Steenkamp began modeling when she was 14. She won contests and eventually appeared in *FHM* as a cover girl. In 2011, South African *FHM* readers were polled, placing her as #40 in the "*FHM* 100 Sexiest Women in the World" poll. In 2012, she also appeared as a celebrity contestant on the BBC Lifestyle show *Baking Made Easy*. Steenkamp was an advocate for women's rights. In November 2012, she began dating South African Olympic and Paralympic runner Oscar Pistorius, who became known as "the fastest man with no legs." He shot her four times while she was hiding in the bathroom of his home.

26

Hello, Darlings! Diana Vreeland here. My, oh, my, what an honor this is! I am eager to begin.

Fashion. The fashion life! Oh, how I swoon over the fashion life—even from here in the Light, where our fashion is quite different, yet no less grand!

Grand fashion! That is what I strove for in my lifetime as Diane. Grand fashion that elevated the outer person while it also elevated the inner person—and the psyche! For fashion truly is an inside job, as I've heard said here. For fashion—being fashionable—does influence a person's entire person—inside and out!

What should you do if you don't feel the fashion urge? If you don't feel a push to be as fashionable as possible? Well, I daresay this isn't you, if you are reading this book! For most likely, those reading this are quite fashionable—and even slaves to fashion at times. But you may have others in your life who are not of the fashionable sense. And they may exasperate you with their obvious disregard for the finer things in life—or even the necessities—like shoes that do shine and aren't scuffed up like a child's old toy! I say this somewhat in jest, yet I know that this does irk you as a fashionista!

What do I have to say about this? Forget about it!!! Just do!!! For the true answer here is not that you worry about what others are wearing—unless you've been officially tasked with clothing them or critiquing or influencing their attire—but that you worry about what you are wearing. For you are inside of you—your own skin. And you will feel how you look and look how you feel. I know this may not seem to make sense on one level, but on the other level it most certainly makes perfect sense!

Am I suggesting that you don't try to improve the fashion world? Most certainly not! For a fashionista's work is truly never done! I am suggesting that you swallow your ego a bit when you do see a "fashion statement" that makes your eyes nearly pop out of their sockets in disbelief, and that you go on with your day in your own fashionable way. Think of it as you would music if you were a musician, which you just might be! There are those songs and tunes that will make you wish to plug your ears. But to others it is music in their ears!! I think you see of what I speak!

At any rate, what was it like for me as a fashion editor? Well, as you might suspect, my opinions did matter. Sometimes a great deal! Those opinions did hold great weight, and they did impress people, and sway many. In many ways, it was a rather heady job—for I found myself setting fashions, or at least setting the trends that would then lead to the fashions. And that was a remarkable thing! In fact, I am still doing the same here in and from the Light. Setting the stage for trends that will eventually follow suit with fabulous, utterly divine fashions! I have to say to you now, if you are wondering, that the fun just doesn't stop when it comes to fashion, fashion, fashion! Unlike the conventional wisdom there on Earth, you will take your fashion to the grave. LOL, as you say!

Now on to shoes before I leave you. Oh, my, there are some rather odd contraptions on which people walk nowadays! I do say so!! But once again, if you feel good in what you are wearing on your feet— hooray! But if you think, as a fashion designer, that you could do better in the shoe realm, then I do urge you to call on yours truly. I'll be glad to give you some tips for some utterly divine looking shoes that are also ultra-comfortable, as they might say! And for yourself, please do shine your shoes, and keep them clean. I do know that people walk about in their shoes thinking that they are, well, shoes, and therefore will get dirty. While that is true, it is also true that people will and do look at your feet and your shoes. And if your shoes are dull or dirty or torn or ripped, then that does give them an impression of you!

Yes, it is a fact. Though not always a welcome one. When people first meet you, they will judge you by the clothes on your back—and front— ha ha! So, do think of that when you wish to impress someone(s). Okay! And if you do need a little assist when it comes to choosing the perfect outfit, call on yours truly! I will be at your side in a flash, happy to help you pick out the perfect wardrobe—shoes and all!

Do enjoy the magic of the fashion world!
Yours Truly and Forever,
Diana Vreeland

DIANA VREELAND was a fashion columnist and editor born on September 29, 1903. She died at the age of 85, due to a heart attack, on August 22, 1989. Vreeland was well-known as a "genius" fashion editor. She was also known as the "high priestess of fashion." Vreeland served as fashion editor of *Harper's Bazaar* from 1937 to 1962, and then jumped to *Vogue*, where she was editor-in-chief until 1971. After that she started staging annual fashion show exhibitions that drew millions of visitors to New York City from around the world. She also worked as a special consultant for the Costume Institute of the Metropolitan Museum of Art. In 1964, Vreeland was placed on the International Best Dressed List Hall of Fame. Known for her keen eye for fashion, many designers report that she gave them important exposure that helped launch their careers. Vreeland stayed fashionably thin. She was said to dine on oatmeal and tea for breakfast while she worked in bed. She'd report to the office about noon. It was during her period working for the museum that she became the voice of the fashion world. She was sought after as an attendee at parties and fashion openings. She received awards from many organizations, including the Rhode Island School of Design. She also became a chevalier of the French National Order of Merit.

———∞———

"Unshined shoes are the end of civilization."

"Style—all who have it share one thing: originality."

"I loathe narcissism, but I approve of vanity."
      —Diane Vreeland

27

❧ WILHELMINA COOPER ❧

*Hello! Quite happy to present! Wilhelmina Cooper here. I'm excited,
as they say, to share my tidbits about fashion, as they are!*

Modeling. Modeling fashions. Modeling divine fashion, fashion,
fashion! Oh, my, what a wondrous thing! I did so enjoy
modeling. But, to be truthful, I did enjoy finding and mentoring and
guiding models even more. That was a wondrous occupation. And
quite a grand calling! For it does take a certain soul to be able to spot
talent—often raw—and to guide the model as he or she does come
into his or her own. This is especially a feat in the world in which you
live. It most certainly is!

What of this? What of modeling and the world in which you live? Certainly, some could tell you that modeling is "not like it used to be." While
others will tell you that the modeling profession today is so much better than
it used to be. That it was limiting "back in the day," so to speak.

While I am not here to "argue" either way, I am here to tell you that
modeling is a most revered profession—considered a highly evolved
occupation from here in the Light. That might surprise you, as you
might be thinking that certainly modeling is quite frivolous to be of
much consequence in the ether. But the truth is that we do take
modeling and the fashions that models display quite seriously. For to be
at one with the idea of displaying the human form and the very essence
of human beauty—that is truly a calling! And a high honor at that.

How is this so? You may be asking yourself or us.

Here is the thing, as you say now in your day. Beauty is beauty is beauty is beauty. Certainly, beauty is what one might wear, and beauty is a look in one's eyes, and beauty is in a pair of well-crafted shoes, and beauty is in a baby's smile. Beauty is a quite individual thing, and yet beauty is a quite universal thing. For we all have our own standards of beauty, most certainly. But we all do enjoy beauty for beauty's sake. There isn't a person, place or thing that is not called beautiful in one form or another. And there is not a person on the Earth Plane who doesn't consider at least one thing in the world beautiful. Most likely many things.

And now I shall digress. How did I choose my models? How did I know that a model would do quite well with the profession—shine even? Well, for one, I could tell by the gleam in her eyes. A model who shall go far has a hunger in the eyes—to be sure—and at the same time she has a knowing in her eyes that she will succeed, no matter what happens. It is just a matter of time—that is all.

What else? Well, I did look for models who could control themselves. Control their frustration and impatience, as well as the frustration and impatience of those wishing something from them. I also sought out models who had positive as their defaults. Certainly, you all have your ups and your downs, and that is to be expected, but the models who got up and dusted themselves off and tried again soon after "failing," those were the models I did seek out. I also put my attention toward models who refrained from requiring some sort of consolation from others when they "failed." Rather, I looked for models who could effectively "self-soothe" and move on with their careers. Those who could and did know that all was as it should be, and that they were the ones in charge of their own lives.

Was this hard to find in a model—this last attribute? Most certainly! And I didn't always find that attribute in every girl I signed on. But when I did. When I found those models, who knew intrinsically that it was their birthright to be models and that they were beautiful through and through, and refused to let others push through their boundaries, I knew I had models who could go the distance. Such models truly did and do become stars. And as the captains of their own ships, they reach the finish line again and again. They also enjoy successful lives as models. Greatly revered ones.

> *That's all for me right now. I do thank you for listening. And if you wish to be a model, I do encourage you to embrace your "awesomeness" and proceed to model with the knowledge and the knowing that you will go far!*
>
> *Good Day to You,*
> *Wilhelmina Cooper*

WILHELMINA GERTRUD FRIEDA COOPER was a Dutch-American model and modeling agent born on May 1, 1939. She died at the age of 40, due to lung cancer, on March 1, 1980. Cooper is known for founding Wilhelmina Models, which is still in existence today. Cooper was born in the Netherlands, the daughter of a butcher. After World War II, the family moved to Germany; then immigrated to Chicago in 1954. Cooper soon became a well-known model, starting with Ford Models. During her modeling career, which spanned the 1950s and 1960s, she appeared on the cover of 255 magazines—including holding a record for appearing on *American Vogue* 28 times. She also modeled in Europe and worked for Christian Dior (#33) and Coco Chanel (#6). She married Victor Bruce Cooper in 1965, and they founded Wilhelmina Models in 1967 in New York City. They had two children.

28

➤ L'WREN SCOTT ➤

Hi there! L'Wren Scott here. Really, really honored and excited to present! Let's get to it, as they say!

Perfume. A signature scent. That is one of the things I would like to discuss today. One's signature scent. That can most certainly come forth in a most divine perfume! Oh, how many perfumes are out there available today! Back in my day, which wasn't in the too distant past, perfumes were as plentiful as now. However, perfumes weren't as refined as today.

Certainly, there weren't the perfume manufacturers putting as much research and time and energy into studying scents and into making scents smell so wonderfully and into making scents endure. For there are those perfumes that you may put on that do seem to disappear as if in a whiff of smoke! And then there are those perfumes that last.

Today's perfume manufacturers and creators do use sommeliers, so to speak, for the perfumes. Certainly, they have their own name, these perfume "smellers." That of perfumer or aromachologist, or "nose," to be crasser. But in many ways, these terms don't accurately or completely describe what a person, who does smell and create and dream up and theorize perfumes, does. Certainly, such a person is a sommelier of scents! For he or she does smell the scents to see what will land lightly, yet memorably on the nose and in the olfactory system. At the same time, such a person will think of and look to how that scent might combine with the skin of the person, as well as how that person wishes to feel when he or she uses the scent.

For feelings, Dear Fashion Mavens and Men, are a huge part of scents. Scents do evoke memories. They most certainly do! And scents therefore do evoke a plethora of feelings when those memories are accessed.

Of course, women and men wish to feel good when they use certain scents. Certainly, they wish to feel as if they are flying high and feeling ultra-good, generally speaking! So that is a big consideration when dreaming up and creating and executing scents, and then passing them on to the public.

This all being said, please do consider the role of scents as you go about your days in the fashion world, and most certainly as you choose the perfumes you wish to perfume your person with!

Okay, I shall say a few words about other fashion items here, as I was a fashion designer! What would you like to hear about? Purses perhaps? Or shoes? Or skirts? Or dresses? Or evening gowns?

I shall talk a bit about evening gowns. Though I do love all those other topics!

Evening gowns. How delicious are they! For they do make one feel like swooning a bit, even to look at, wouldn't you agree? And they do offer a perfect opportunity for every woman who wears them to feel like Cinderella! Or sleeping Beauty! Or Rapunzel! You can insert your favorite fairytale princess here!

What else shall I tell you about evening gowns? Well, if you are to choose one for yourself or a client, do go for all that glitters—yet in a most entrancing way! But most importantly, do go for what makes the person feel like a princess, or queen! For that is what this is all about. Evening gowns making one feel special and like no other being in the world!

In fact, all fashion is about this one little big thing. Making oneself feel special and making oneself feel magical, even! That, my Dear

Enlightened Fashion Lovers, is what dear fashion, fashion, fashion is all about!

Good Day to You! I am, once again, honored. And do thank you for listening, ever so much!
Yours Kindly,
L' Wren Scott

———— ∞∞∞ ————

LAURA "LUANN" BAMBROUGH (L' Wren Scott) was an American fashion designer and stylist born on April 28, 1964. She died at the age of 49, due to suicide, on March 17, 2014. Scott, who was raised by adoptive Mormon parents in Utah, started as a model in Paris. In the early 1990s, she moved to California and became a stylist. L' Wren initially worked with photographer Herb Ritts, eventually also working with Karl Lagerfeld (#12) and others. She created the iconic ad campaign for Elizabeth Taylor's White Diamonds perfume, which became the most well-known celebrity scent ever. Scott styled a variety of celebrities, including Madonna and Julia Roberts. She also designed costumes for movies, including *Ocean's Thirteen* and *Eyes Wide Shut*. Scott moved from styling to fashion designing, becoming known for creating a look that epitomized "luxury dressing." She took a hands-on approach, often cutting patterns, sewing, and fitting clothes. Scott was involved in a long-term relationship with The Rolling Stone's lead singer, Mick Jagger, whom she met in Paris in 2001. She had been suffering from depression prior to her death.

29

❧ JHERI REDDING ❧

Hello! Thanks much for listening. Jheri Redding here. Come to share about the beautiful world of beauty! Hooray!

What shall I tell you about beauty, beauty, beauty? Well, you most likely know that beauty and the beauty industry and helping to make people beautiful and beautifying yourself is a most glorious calling. For truly, it certainly is a calling. If you feel that you are called to help people beautify themselves, well, then, you most certainly are!

In my life as Jheri that was my calling. I did start out as a chemist, but that was only done to further my grand pursuit and to guide and fuel it. And my grand pursuit was within the realm of beauty and helping oneself attain great heights in this area. I do think you know of what I speak. And if you don't, prepare to be enlightened!

What shall we speak of? What shall we discuss—us here in the Light Plane's Fashion School, and you in the Earth Plane's Fashion School?

How about this? How about if you take a few minutes to access your true fashion self? How about if you try meditating a bit on what it is you would like to do with your time on Earth in the Fashion World? Do close your eyes and take a big breath. Then envision a giant white board in your mind's eye. Simply wait until fashions or ideas of fashions or ideas about fashion enter the white board. You might see a beautiful dress like no other come swirling onto the white board stage! Or you may see yourself holding a discourse with fashion students as an instructor. Or you may see yourself designing and styling fabulous hairstyles for all the world to try and enjoy!!!!

Whatever it is that does walk onto the white board in your mind's eye is most certainly something that your soul wishes to explore in this lifetime right here and now. Could that change next year or tomorrow or next week? Of course! For you are on the Earth Plane right now to enjoy all that the Earth Plane has to offer—including fabulous, glorious, stupendous fashion!

Okay, I hear you asking, when is he going to talk about hair? For hair was certainly his forte. I will verify that that is correct! It was my forte as Jheri, most certainly! And it will continue to be here in the Light. At the same time, I have had other lives in the fashion industry. For when fashion does seep into your very pores, so to speak, it just doesn't leave!!! You will find if you have a fashion sense now that you most certainly have always had one. And hooray for that!

Back to the matter at hand. Hair. And speaking of hand. Isn't it absolutely divine when hair is felt in the hands? When hair is teased out by the hands? When hair is caressed by the hands? I say all this now, because I would like to suggest something. I know this doesn't necessarily go with the styles that do need a lacquer of sorts in terms of hairspray—but for those of you who wear your hair naturally styled, like Dear Julie, and don't spray on a ton of hairspray—do run your hands through your hair at least once a day. Do! For when you do, you infuse your hair with intention. That is, intention that you know your hair is lovely—no matter how little or how much you have—and that you intend to give your hair as much love and attention as possible!

For that is what hair truly needs. Lots of TLC. I know another expert here has mentioned avocados and avocado oil for the hair, and I will repeat it. I will also add to eat avocados and other vegetables that contain the same compounds. For that will make your hair lustrous!!!

What else? Watch the heat on the hair. You dears know this, but it bears repeating. And watch the alcohol consumption. It does create drying in the hair. Dryness can be problematic—causing a sort of crisping and splitting.

That's all from me for now! I am honored to have presented, and I wish you a glorious time enjoying yourselves in the Earth Plane's Beauty school. I shall see you in the Light!
    Yours Truly,
    Jheri Redding

JHERI REDDING was an American hairdresser, chemist, and haircare products creator and businessman born on March 2, 1907. He died at the age of 91 on March 15, 1998. Known as the "Godfather of Hair," Redding is credited as being the inventor of the modern-day hair conditioner, and for being the first to put vitamins and minerals into haircare products. He also created pH balanced shampoos that match the mild acidity of human skin. Born on a farm in Illinois to Irish immigrant farmers, Redding was one of the first men in his home state to become licensed in cosmetology. He did this during the Great Depression, because he saw hairdressers making more money than farmers. Prior to getting his license, Redding was a chemistry and physics teacher. The chemistry came in handy when he became a hairdresser, because he was never satisfied with available haircare products. This prompted him to begin experimenting with various chemicals and items in the kitchen, such as mayonnaise. The research eventually led to Jheri Redding haircare products, such as shampoos, conditioners, and styling creams and gels. He also revolutionized perming hair with the introduction of the Jheri Curl. Redding founded four haircare companies: Jheri Redding Products, Redken, which he co-founded with Paul Kent Meehan, and the Jhirmack Company and Nexxus. A charismatic presenter and speaker, Redding would mesmerize audiences of all sizes with his explanations of the chemistry of hair and the importance of using high-quality haircare products. For instance, he would stick litmus paper in his products, and they would show golden depicting pH-balanced, while other products showed black. He mentored many in the haircare industry.

30

⇥ CAROLE LITTLE ⇤

Hello! Carole Little here. Very excited for this opportunity! Let's get to it, as they say!

Oh, my, what a glorious opp! I am excited, as I said, to share my take from here in the Light on fashion and beauty. Oh, my!

Dresses. Of all fashions, including accessories, I have to say that dresses are on the top of my list of favorites.

What is it about dresses? Certainly, it is the flow of the dress. It is the ease by which a dress falls on a woman's (or man's) body, and it is the ease at which the dress can make its way through all manner of obstacles. By that I mean that dresses flow. And dresses can flow so well that they do flatter the figure. They also flow as you walk, as if you are walking on air, even. You can just as easily walk through a hallway in a dress as you can walk through a garden in one. They fit just about anywhere!

Am I suggesting that dresses do bring a bit of magic to one's persona and one's life? I certainly am! For dresses are etheric to a certain degree. And they do have fun written all over them. Fun, fun, fun! That is just about what dresses do say. Of course, there are the dresses that spell ELEGANCE in giant letters. And they are quite divine. At the same time, however, you will see that even elegance can spell fun.

It is the freeing nature of dresses that helps make them magical. There are less constraints than other types of clothing. With fewer limiting constraints you will find that a person's mood lightens. And creativity seems to flow when one wears a dress. (Case in point: Julie is wearing a dress as she channels this. No surprise there!)

What else about dresses that makes them so perfect and so ethereal and so entrancing even?

The material. There are so many materials that make for fabulous dresses. You have silk, of course, and cotton, and rayon, and you can even make a dress with burlap, though I wouldn't advise it! The point is that you can use just about any type of cloth to make a dress, and it will turn out quite well!

Am I saying that it's hard to make a "bad" dress? In a way, yes. For the flow and the freedom of dresses does make it difficult to make a dress that no one would want to wear. Certainly, if it doesn't have all the qualities of a "good" dress, then few people may want to wear it. However, I can assure you that someone or more than someone is going to like the dress and want to wear it. You've most likely noticed that fact in the dresses that are worn on the proverbial red carpet!

But I digress. Back to dresses and their beauty and what makes them the most divine of the fashion elements.

Here is something to ponder and chew over. How do you feel in a dress? You may find that you just feel different when you wear a dress. The fact is that wearing a dress does punctuate things for people. It does make things seem a bit richer. In fact, wearing a dress may make you feel as if you've just put a big exclamation point after your fashion for that day. You may feel freer in a dress—which we do know Julie does feel. You may also feel even more lovely. You could even feel like a princess in a dress! And that is absolutely divine. For dresses, we can tell you from here in the Light, were made to make your life feel like a fairytale!

Please do go ahead and experiment with dresses. Try a bunch of dresses on. Feel the fabric on your skin. Do take a few twirls in the mirror to see how the dresses flow and look when you do this. For that is important as well! And part of the princess fairytale existence.

Before you go, one more thing about dresses that makes them even more glorious. You can wear dresses at absolutely any age. For they have the added benefit of having a wide variety of lengths.

Go for it!!! Wear dresses, dresses, dresses with abandon. You shall be glad you did!

That's all from me for now.
Good Day to You and Your Dresses!
Carole Little

P.S. I do know that I was known for my fashionable work attire. Dresses fit into this vein, as well. And they are delightfully refreshing on a hot, hot day! Yet equally as comfy on a cold one.

———— ∞∞ ————

CAROLE LITTLE was an American fashion designer born on September 27, 1934. She died at the age of 80, due to cancer, on September 19, 2015. Little is known for creating California chic affordable sportswear, which was embraced by working women. Her clothing featured signature mixed prints and was comfortable, often loose-fitting, and could easily be mixed and matched. Born in Chicago to a Sears shoe executive, Little and her family moved to Los Angeles when she was a child. She studied at UCLA, majoring in English, and then studied fashion design at Los Angeles Trade Technical College. Her first job in the fashion industry was for a swimsuit maker. She also worked for a manufacturer of trendsetting clothing, including hot pants. In 1974, Little formed the company California Fashion Industries with Leonard Rabinowitz, whom she later married. They used money borrowed from his parents. Though the company originally lost money, when the Carole Little brand appeared in *People* magazine featuring model Lauren Hutton on the cover wearing a silk blouse, business increased substantially and continued to do so. The company reached $350 million by the early 1990s.

31

➤ Miles Cahn ❦

Hello! Miles Cahn here. Delighted to present! Founder of Coach (leather goods galore!) Let us do go on now!

Oh, purses, purses, purses, and leather accessories—like leather ties for a "cowboy" attire, and leather belts, and leather wallets, and then back to leather purses. What a delight is leather! For it is so durable, and yet it has a look to it that can be quite light looking and light to the touch. Especially treated leather that has been made to be as soft as butter! Oh, my! Fresh leather purses and freshly prepared leather. The aroma is intoxicating! It spells new, as it also spells adventure!

Wouldn't you agree that purses do spell adventure? For who knows where you shall take them? And who knows who shall compliment you on your brand new, or well-used glorious purse! Think of all the adventures purses do have! For they do see you at your absolute best. When you are dressed up to go out on the town, and when you are dressed to the hilt to impress for a job interview!

And then, let us do face it, purses do see you at your absolute worst, wouldn't you say? They see you when you've had a bad day and are a bit grumpy. And they do see you when you have gotten some bad news. They most certainly see you up close and personal when you are digging around in them for a tissue for teary eyes, or when you are digging around for the lipstick you just know is in there!

Julie even knows a dear girl who throws her wedding ring into her purse when she's gardening or partaking in other potentially dirty work. The wedding ring does roll around in there until she fishes it out! And then there are all the candies and candy wrappers located in the purse!

Oh, the places purses do go. And the things you experience with your purse. In many respects, purses are a sort of security blanket for women and some men. And for that reason, they must be the absolute best they can be. Wouldn't you agree?

So, if you are thinking about buying a purse, then do look for a high-quality one, if possible. One that will stand the test of time. For here is the absolute truth! If you fall in love with a purse, you do want it to withstand all your travels. You do want it not to fall apart at the first signs of use. Of course, older purses will show some wear over time, but wear is most definitely different than coming apart at the seams and having zipper closing issues, and unusual fading. I think you see what I mean!

Of course, if you do find a purse that you absolutely must have, even though the workmanship is a bit questionable, then do go for it! Think about using the purse less frequently than you would otherwise, so as not to wear it out too soon! Use it for those special occasions when you wish to have a bit of zing, or when you wish a bit of color, or when you just want to have some good old fun!

For that certainly is what purses are all about. Yes, they are functional. And you do want them to have ample storage and plenty of compartments to ensure that you stay organized, if you so choose. But you also just want to have fun with purses, purses, purses! For few accessories, truly, are as fun as the delightful purse!

Good day to you always! And a good night, too! I wish you much fun with purses. And if you choose to make purses, please do keep my tips here in mind. Make them fashionable, of course. Make them functional, of course. Make them well made, of course. And make them delightfully fun, fun, fun!

    Sincerely Yours,
    Miles Cahn

MILES CAHN was an American businessman and designer born on April 18, 1921. He died at the age of 95 on February 10, 2017. Miles is known for co-founding the Coach Leatherware Company, known as Coach Inc., with his wife Lillian Cahn. The company helped redefine the American handbag as something practical, yet fashionable. One of their signature purses is the shopping bag purse. It was modeled after a shopping bag Lillian used to make food deliveries for her family's business during the Depression. The Cahns founded Coach in 1961 after they bought a wallet manufacturer in New York City. It was Lillian's suggestion to create purses out of cowhide used to make baseball gloves. Miles was said to think the idea silly at first, because many stores were simply selling European knockoffs at the time. But Lillian insisted. They made colorful, practical leather bags that soon became popular amongst upscale women across the US. The bags cost thousands today. Miles was born in New York to parents who had fled to the US from Russia during the Russian Revolution. He went to City College in New York and served during World War II in the Army. The couple originally met in New York City and married in 1947. After selling Coach in 1985 for $30 million, the couple started a farm where they made goat cheese. They sold the farm in 2006. Lillian died in 2013 at the age of 89.

32

≫ ANNE KLEIN ≪

Anne Klein here. Pleased to present. Let us begin, for I have quite a bit to say! And I am highly honored to have squeezed in here second to last!

What shall you wear? Truly, what shall you wear? How many times have you said that to yourself? How many times have you worried about that very question? Looking here, there and everywhere in your mind as you wonder what on earth you could have in your closet or drawers that would be perfect for the occasion you have in mind. Certainly, you wrack your brain about the rack of clothes in your bedroom!

Is there something perfect to wear for each occasion? Some might say otherwise, but I would say yes! There most certainly is! And you lovely fashionistas do find just the perfect things to wear. I do applaud you for having the stick-to-it-ness that it does take to find the absolutely best outfit for every occasion!

Does this take a bit of work and ingenuity? Yes, it does! Those of you who do this know that it does. And yet, I would bet, if I were a betting woman, that you do enjoy just about every moment of the planning and dreaming, and the creative juices do flow. And then you enjoy the Eureka moment when you pair this with that and that with this and come up with the most divine outfit! I have to add a hooray here, for that is most certainly what occurs when this does happen!

Speaking of finding the right outfit. How about shopping? I don't believe that anyone has talked about this here. And so, I shall!

Shopping truly is a treasure hunt. Wouldn't you agree? It's something that does get your blood flowing and your heart racing. At times, I do remember as Anne that I would feel such a rush that it felt as if my hearing would disappear for a bit. That was okay, because you truly don't need to hear your clothing as you choose it. But it was a rather odd sensation. I do know now that it was the endorphins coursing through me at the delight I had in shopping! It truly is an aphrodisiac of sorts and quite addictive. That being said, I do urge you to try it, if you haven't already. But I'm guessing that you've already tried it many a time, and that you truly do adore shopping! I have to say now that I am here that shopping is a truly honorable "sport" of sorts! Quite a wondrous hobby! So, do be proud of yourself if you are a shopping guru or ninja! For that does take some practice, and it does take some gumption, and it does take some creativity, and it does take oodles of stamina!

What else shall I impart? Do think about your jewelry. For jewelry does adorn your outfits, and jewelry is a sort of badge of honor. By that I mean that the right jewelry can make you appear as a princess or queen. And at the very least, a quite savvy dresser and shopper!

The quality of your jewelry is a point of contention for many. I do urge you to pay special attention if you are talking about family heirlooms or expensive pieces, but I do suggest that you have a bit of fun with costume jewelry. And that you do give it a try—a whirl—if you haven't already. For it can be quite versatile in its own right. It can give you color, and it can give you bling, and it can give you something fun and fancy all at the same time. You can also wear about your neck or in your ears or on your wrist a conversation starter! Julie has some cat earrings that her sister gave her that do swing rather sillily. And then there is the cute-as-a-button necklace that her daughter made her when she was 8! So do go for costume jewelry at times. If you don't want to use it when you are dressed up, do try it when you are looking your casual best or "roughing" it a bit!

Okay, I have rattled on quite a bit. But I do hope you've enjoyed my ramblings and musings about the absolutely stupendous world of fashion, fashion, fashion—as many here have said!
Good shopping to you always!
Anne Klein

———⟨∞⟩———

HANNAH GOLOFSKY (Anne Klein) was an American fashion designer born on August 3, 1923. She died at the age of 50, due to breast cancer, on March 19, 1974. Klein discovered her love of design while in high school. She went to work in the garment making industry after she graduated and attended the Traphagen School of Design in New York from 1937 to 1938. In 1948, she married Ben Klein, who had recently opened the clothing company, Junior Sophisticates. She took on the role of head designer for the company, and the label did well. She designed apparel for women who were small-sized like her. The label allowed for choice between styles, which was a new concept. Like Coco Chanel before her, she used ideas from menswear and added a feminine touch to them. She launched a line of separates in the 1950s, also a new concept. The idea was to be able to put the clothing items in the collection together to make different outfits. Klein participated in The Battle of Versailles Fashion Show in 1973, a year before she died.

33

⇜ CHRISTIAN DIOR ⇝

Christian Dior here! At your humble service. Thank you for reading. And thank you ever so much for adoring fashion!

Fashion! The very essence of fashion is so endearing and something to be utterly and unequivocally adored! For we in the fashion world—and that means you, too—do adore fashion. Now don't we?

How is it possible that everyone doesn't adore the divine world of fashion? You might ask yourself this at times. My answer to this is, don't bother! For those who are meant to adore fashion will most certainly do so. And those who don't, well, they just won't! Until the day comes when they do need to look their absolute best. And then, what do you know! Suddenly, they are interested in fashion. In mixing and matching fashionable attire and those items that do go together when you do put together a good fashion ensemble!

What am I saying here? That everyone in some shape or form or other at one point or many in their lives will most certainly see the divine beauty and the divine honor in fashion, fashion, fashion, as I've seen said here many a time! Yes!

Fashion in itself is a most delightful occupation. And fashion is a most delightful "hobby" or obsession, even. Fashion is one of the finer arts in life. This I would like to impart to you right here and right now!

That being said, please don't ever consider yourself "shallow" or "insipid," even, for your love of fashion. Do drown out the naysayers in that area! For fashion is an admirable profession. And fashion is coming directly from the Light. I assure you! The ideas you get regarding what to wear and what to design and produce are coming from one or many of us here. And from your own creative sensibilities, of course!

What more shall I tell you, being the last one in line here to speak of the glorious world of fashion?

How about I tell you to go ahead and revel in fashion. In fact, put it on like you would a mink coat or stole, and do feel the ultra-luxurious, invigorating, and soothing feelings you do get from this. Go ahead and revel in fashion, fashion, fashion.

If you are inclined to enter the world of fashion—please do so—sooner than later! For the fashion industry so needs a creative soul—genius—like you! We in the Light, as has been mentioned, are most assuredly ready and waiting to help you with the endeavor.

Isn't it marvelous, too, how many ways today you can express your fashion sense and you can share it with the world? You can do so through shoes and handbags and other accessories, just as well as you can do it through evening gowns and casual and business attire. And then there is jewelry and perfumes and household goods that do light up and enliven a home. Truly, if you choose the world of fashion as your occupation, there is an endless treasure trove of options from which to choose! There truly is!

So, do go ahead and enjoy fashion in its many forms. And do tell others of this glorious book full of fashionable advice about fashion from us fashion experts in the Light. We would be most honored and grateful if you do.

See you soon—in your dreams about fashion! And thank you once again for listening.
   Yours Forever,
   Christian Dior

CHRISTIAN DIOR was a French fashion designer born on January 21, 1905. He died at the age of 52, due to a heart attack, on October 24, 1957. Dior is known for founding one of the world's most famous top fashion houses. His fashions continue to influence the international fashion industry. In 1947, Dior entered the Paris fashion scene. His designs went against wartime restrictions and focused on luxury women's fashions. He became one of the most successful fashion designers in the world, due to his designs and business acumen. Dior's designs have been worn by royalty and film stars. He was born in northern France in 1905, the second of five children of a successful fertilizer manufacturer. Dior's family moved to Paris when he was a boy. Although Dior showed a passion for art, his father talked him into studying political science with the idea of him becoming a diplomat. After graduating in 1928, Dior opened a small art gallery instead. During his time as a gallery owner, Dior displayed work from greats such as Pablo Picasso and Max Jacob. He had to close the gallery in 1931, because his mother and older brother died that year and his father's business collapsed. After the gallery closed, he sold fashion sketches to make ends meet. In 1935, he got a job illustrating a magazine. A few years later, he was hired as a design assistant for Paris couturier Robert Piguet. World War II began the following year, and Dior served in the south of France as an officer in the French Army. After France surrendered to Germany in 1940, Dior went back to Paris. He worked for couturier Lucien LeLong for a time. Then in 1946, Dior founded his own fashion house. He was said to be a master at creating captivating silhouettes and shapes. Women protested initially to his designs, which often covered up their legs. They were unused to this after the rations on fabric during the war. Dior appeared on the cover of *Time* magazine in 1957 several months before his death.

If you enjoyed this book by Julie Bawden-Davis, please leave a review on Amazon.com, or any online book or media site, including GoodReads. Your reviews make a world of difference and are greatly appreciated!

About the Channeled Masters Series

The Channeled Masters Series consists of books written from various groups of individuals speaking from within the Light on specific topics. Book #1 is *Channeled Writing Tips from 111 Literary Masters*. Book #2 is *Channeled Cooking Tips from 44 Culinary Masters*. Book #3 is *Channeled Music Tips from 77 Musical Masters*. The next book in the series (#5) is *Channeled Art Tips from 99 Artistic Masters*. It is scheduled for release in early 2020.

Stay Enlightened

Dear Enlightened Reader,

Thanks for reading! Let's stay in touch. In appreciation of you, I post updates, insider information, and sneak peeks of upcoming books on my website at www.juliebawdendavis.com/spiritual-coaching. You can also email me at Julie@JulieBawdenDavis.com, follow me on my Welcome to Ascension page on Facebook, and find me on Amazon.

Even better, you can join my VIP Enlightened Reader's mailing list here (eepurl.com/doM3-X) for weekly Divinely Inspired Channeled Messages just for you.

About the Author

Julie Bawden-Davis is a Southern California professional author, whose work has appeared in a wide variety of publications since 1985. She is also an IMPART certified medium, psychic, and healer (Reiki Master and Karuna Reiki® II Practitioner). A Master Channeler, Julie imparts messages from Spirit/The Light, including through books, written letters, and voice. She is author of *Channeled Writing Tips from 111 Literary Masters, Channeled Cooking Tips from 44 Culinary Masters, Channeled Music Tips from 77 Musical Masters,* and *Channeled Fashion Tips from 33 Master Designers and Models.*

Julie also connects people with their past lives and lends insight as to how those lives relate to this life. Guided by Spirit, Julie heals and redirects past life experiences that are holding people back in this lifetime.

INDEX

www.ingramcontent.com/pod-product-compliance
Lightning Source LLC
LaVergne TN
LVHW011202080426
835508LV00007B/558